AF600639

THE CATHOLIC UNIVERSITY OF AMERICA
CANON LAW STUDIES
No. 235

# The Mass and Holy Communion: Interritual Law

COMMENTARY WITH HISTORICAL NOTES

BY THE
REVEREND JOSEPH ARTHUR HENRY, A.B., J.C.L.
*Priest of the Archdiocese of Philadelphia*

A DISSERTATION

*Submitted to the Faculty of the School of Canon Law of the Catholic University of America in Partial Fulfillment of the Requirements for the Degree of Doctor of Canon Law*

THE CATHOLIC UNIVERSITY OF AMERICA
WASHINGTON, D. C.
1946

*Nihil Obstat:*

JOSEPH A. M. QUIGLEY, J.C.D.,
*Censor Librorum.*

*Philadelphiae, die 3 maii, 1946.*

*Imprimatur:*

✠ D. CARD. DOUGHERTY,
*Archiepiscopus Philadelphiensis.*

*Philadelphiae, die 3 maii, 1946.*



Printed by
THE PAULIST PRESS
401 WEST 59TH STREET
NEW YORK 19, N. Y.

81

TO

MY MOTHER

AND

FATHER

# TABLE OF CONTENTS

CHAPTER IV



CHAPTER V

## FOREWORD

It is stated in the first canon of the Code of Canon Law that the laws of the Code regard only the Latin Church and do not bind the Oriental Church except in those matters which of their very nature also affect the Oriental Church. Among the canons of the Code which treat of the Sacrament of the Holy Eucharist there are some canons which affect the Oriental Church as well as the Latin Church. These canons are interritual laws—laws to be observed when a priest of one Rite wishes to celebrate Mass in another Rite, or to distribute Holy Communion consecrated in another Rite, or to perform these functions in a Church of a different Rite; and laws for the faithful who desire to receive Holy Communion in a Rite different from their own.

The present work sketches the history of the development of the laws regarding the celebration of Mass and the distribution of Holy Communion in the different Rites from the Last Supper to the Code of Canon Law (1918), and presents a canonical commentary on the interritual laws which are found in the Code of Canon Law and in the decrees of the Popes, of the Sacred Congregations and of the National and Provincial Synods. It is not intended that this be a liturgical work, yet in the treatment of a subject in which liturgy has a major part it is impossible not to include some references to the liturgy. Emphasis, however, is placed on the legislation affecting the interritual celebration of Mass and distribution of Holy Communion.

The first part of this work deals with the period from the Last Supper to the I Council of Nicaea (325). During that time there were no distinct Rites, but they were in the process of development.

The second part covers the time from the I Council of Nicaea (325) to the Council of Trent (1545-1563). In the beginning of this period the different Rites appear. At first there was a different Rite for almost every episcopal see, but these Rites soon became identified with the Rite of their own Patriarchal city, namely Rome, Alexandria or Antioch. The laws governing the Rites and the differences between the Rites are treated in this second part; the Latin Rite first, then the Oriental. The Great Schism and the Councils of Reunion in their effects on interritual law are also studied.

The third part is a history of the laws enacted after the Council of Trent (1545-1563) to the Code of Canon Law (1918). The legislation during this period came, for the most part, from the various Popes and Sacred Congregations. Many of the laws which were prescribed still obtain today, and some of the laws were incorporated into the Code of Canon Law of the Latin Church. The National and Provincial Synods which were held for the different Oriental Rites also made laws and most of these laws still oblige the faithful of the respective Rites.

The promulgation of the Code marked the beginning of a new era in Canon Law for the Latin Church. The year 1918 is considered as the line of demarcation between the old law and the new law. But following the Councils of Florence (1438-1445) and of Trent (1545-1563), there is not found a precise body of Canon Law for the Oriental Church. The Oriental Church does not as yet have its laws codified, and the faithful of the Oriental Rites are bound not only by the interritual laws of the Code of Canon Law of the Latin Church, but also by the decrees of the Popes, of the Sacred Congregations and of the National and Provincial Synods which were issued before the promulgation of the Code, insofar as they were not expressly abrogated by the Code. The Eastern and Western Church, of course, must also obey the legislation enacted for each Church respectively by the Holy See since the promulgation of the Code.

In addition to the history which is contained in this third part of the development of the interritual laws regarding the celebration of Mass and the distribution of Holy Communion during the period from the Council of Trent (1545-1563) to the Code of Canon Law (1918), it was thought best, then, to include the canonical commentary immediately after the historical synopsis of each law.

The writer wishes to express his sincere gratitude to His Eminence, Dennis Cardinal Dougherty, Archbishop of Philadelphia, for the opportunity to pursue graduate studies in Canon Law at The

Catholic University of America; to the members of the Faculty of the School of Canon Law for their kind assistance and helpful direction during his course at the University; and to all others who contributed by their interest and aid towards the completion of this dissertation.

# Part I

# First Holy Thursday to the I Council of Nicaea (325)

## CHAPTER I

## THE MASS IN THE NEW TESTAMENT

After Our Lord had instituted the Holy Eucharist, the ceremonies and the liturgy of the Mass were in a state of development and subject to further change in detail. In the early Church there were no distinct Rites or Liturgies as they exist today. These appeared later. In the beginning the religious meetings of the people followed the order of the Jewish synagogue service in much of its outward form. When the Holy Eucharist was celebrated, the celebration followed these services, but there was not always a Eucharistic sacrifice at every Christian assembly. In the first century, also, the *Agape* or Love Feast was held, sometimes before and sometimes after the celebration of the Holy Eucharist. Because of abuses, however, the *Agape* disappeared after the first century.[1]

The meetings of the first Christians, then, had some order, but there was a certain freedom with regard to the ceremonies and pray-

[1] 1 Cor., xi, 20-22; Jude, v, 12; Tertullian, *De Jejunio adversus Psychicos,* XVII—*Corpus Scriptorum Ecclesiasticorum Latinorum* [*CSEL*] (Vindobonae: F. Tempsky, 1866—), Vol. XX (ed. Reifferscheid et Wissowa, 1890), 296, and J. P. Migne, *Patrologiae Cursus Completus, Series Latina* [*MPL*] (221 vols., Parisiis, 1844-1864), II, 977. Tertullian, *Apologetica,* XXXIX—*MPL,* I, 470. Cf. Council in Trullo (692), can. 74—Jean Hardouin, *Acta Conciliorum et Epistolae Decretales ac Constitutiones Summorum Pontificum* (12 vols., Parisiis, 1714-1715), III, 1678 (hereafter cited Hardouin), and J. Mansi, *Sacrorum Conciliorum Nova et Amplissima Collectio* (53 vols. in 60, Parisiis, 1901-1927), XI, 975 (hereafter cited Mansi). Cf. also F. X. Funk, *A Manual of Church History* (2 vols., translated by P. Perciballi and edited by W. H. Kent, O.S.C., London: Burns, Oates & Washbourne, Ltd., 1938), I, 65.

ers. The forms of worship and the offering of the Holy Sacrifice differed from church to church. The language, too, differed. The vernacular of the local faithful was the language for the Holy Eucharist.[2] The only elements that were determined were the essential rites which Our Lord Himself handed down through His Apostles with the words: "Do this in remembrance of Me." [3] Without these essential elements, the Holy Eucharist could not be celebrated in any Rite.

The three Synoptic Gospels of St. Matthew, St. Mark and St. Luke together with St. Paul's I Epistle to the Corinthians contain the account of the First Mass celebrated by Our Lord after the Last Supper.[4] Putting these four accounts together, one finds the essential elements of the First Mass celebrated by Our Lord on Holy Thursday to have been the following: Our Lord took bread, gave thanks, blessed it, broke it and gave it to His Apostles with the words: "Take and eat; this is my body." Then He took the cup of wine, gave thanks and gave it to His Apostles and said: "All of you drink of this; for this is my blood of the new covenant, which is being shed for many unto the forgiveness of sins." [5] St. Luke and St. Paul add the words: "Do this in remembrance of me." [6]

The essential elements of the Mass handed down by the New Testament are then: the matter—bread and wine; the form for the bread—"This is my body," for the wine—"This is my blood"; prayers of thanksgiving; breaking of the bread; Communion in both species. The *Acts of the Apostles* mentions that the Mass was celebrated on the first day of the week, namely, on Sunday.[7]

[2] Cf. Donald Attwater, *The Catholic Eastern Churches* (Milwaukee: Bruce Publishing Company, 1937), p. 5. Sévérien Salaville, *An Introduction to the Study of Eastern Liturgies* (London: Sands & Co., 1938), pp. 34, 47 (hereafter cited *Eastern Liturgies*). Cf. also Archdale King, *Notes on the Catholic Liturgies* (New York: Longmans, Green & Co., 1930), pp. 329-331.

[3] St. Luke, xxii, 19; St. Paul, 1 Cor., xi, 24.

[4] Matt., xxvi, 26-29; Mark, xiv, 22-25; Luke, xxii, 19-20; 1 Cor., xi, 23-25.

[5] Matt., xxvi, 26-28.

[6] *Loc. cit.*

[7] Acts, xx, 7.

## CHAPTER II

## PATRISTIC ACCOUNT OF THE CEREMONIES OF THE MASS

DURING the three centuries following the Last Supper the ceremonies of the Mass developed and became more determined. Gradually, too, the forms of worship and of the offering of the Holy Sacrifice solidified into types or families. The liturgy of the most important churches became the norm for the churches of lesser importance associated with and dependent on them. In examining the sources of the first three centuries which contain testimony of the Holy Eucharist, one can follow these developments of the liturgy of the Mass until the eventual appearance of the well defined and distinct Rites.

The first source, after the New Testament, which makes allusion to the Holy Eucharist is the *Didache* (c. 90-100 A.D.). This work contributes to the fund of information regarding the Eucharistic Sacrifice in the early days of the Church the knowledge that the Holy Eucharist was celebrated every Sunday and that confession was made before the receiving of Holy Communion.[1] The *Didache* also gives the name "Eucharist"—εὐχαριστία—to the celebration of the Holy Sacrifice.[2] The matter of the Eucharistic Sacrifice is referred to as the chalice and the bread that was broken, but with no further

[1] C. XIV, n. 1: "Die autem dominica congregati frangite panem et gratias agite, postquam confessi eritis peccata vestra, ut mundum sit sacrificium vestrum."—Johannes Quasten, *Monumenta Eucharistica et Liturgica Vetustissima* (Bonnae: Petrus Hanstein, 1935), pars I, 12 (based on the Funk-Bihlmeyer edition of the *Didache*, 1924). (Hereafter cited Quasten, *Monumenta*.) Cf. Fortescue, *The Mass: A Study of the Roman Liturgy* (New York: Longmans, Green & Co., 1930), p. 8 (hereafter cited *The Mass*); J. Husslein, S.J., *The Mass of the Apostles* (New York: P. J. Kenedy & Sons, 1929), p. 181 (hereafter cited *The Mass*).

[2] C. IX, n. 1—Quasten, *Monumenta*, I, 10: —*De* Περὶ δὲ τῆς εὐχαριστίας *eucharistia*. Cf. Fortescue, *loc. cit.*; Husslein, *ibid.*, p. 184; Duchesne, *Christian Worship: Its Origin and Evolution* (London: Society for Promoting Christian Knowledge, 1903), p. 52 (hereafter cited *Christian Worship*).

qualifications.[3] Communion is given in both species, but only to those who are baptized.[4]

Although the *Didache* mentions bread and wine as the matter of the Holy Eucharist, the I Epistle of Pope St. Alexander I (c. 105-115) adds a new element to those noted in the testimony heretofore presented. Bread and wine are the species offered in the sacrifice, but the wine is mixed with water.[5]

St. Ignatius the Martyr (d. 107) adds his testimony to that of the *Acts of the Apostles* and the *Didache* to confirm the prevalence of the custom that the Sacrifice of the Holy Eucharist should be celebrated on Sunday.[6] St. Ignatius exerted his efforts against the attendance of the Christians at the heretical and schismatical eucharistic services. He emphasized the unity of the Holy Sacrifice against the heretics and schismatics by comparing the unity of the Eucharistic Sacrifice to Our Lord's union with His Father. Since Our Lord did nothing without His Father, so the people should do nothing without the bishop and priests, but should come together to one altar.[7]

In the Epistle to the Smyrneans, St. Ignatius indicates the reason

[3] Quasten, *ibid.*, c. IX, nn. 2-3, 10; Fortescue, *loc. cit.*; Husslein, *loc. cit.*; Duchesne, *loc. cit.*

[4] *Ibid.*, c. IX, n. 5; Quasten, *ibid.*, 11; Fortescue, *loc. cit.*; Husslein, *ibid.*, p. 185; Duchesne, *ibid.*, p. 53.

[5] "In sacramentorum quoque oblationibus, quae inter missarum solemnia Domino offeruntur, passio Domini miscenda est, ut ejus, cujus corpus et sanguis conficitur, passio celebretur, ita ut, repulsis opinionibus superstitionum panis tantum et vinum aqua permixtum in sacrificia offerantur. Non debet enim (ut a Patribus accepimus, et ipsa ratio docet) in calice Domini aut vinum solum aut aqua sola offerri, sed utrumque ex latere ejus in passione sua profluxisse legitur."—Mansi, I, 638, n. iv; Philippus Jaffé, *Regesta Pontificum Romanorum ab condita Ecclesia ad annum post Christum natum MCXCVIII (1198)* (2. ed., cura Wattenbach, Kaltenbrunner [ad annum 590], Ewald [anno 590-882], Löwenfeld [anno 882-1198], 2 vols., Lipsiae, 1885-1888), n. 24 (hereafter cited Jaffé).

[6] *Epistola ad Magnesios,* IX, 1—Migne, *Patrologiae Cursus Completus, Series Graeca* [*MPG*] (161 vols. in 164, Parisiis, 1856-1866), V, 669. Cf. Fortescue, *The Mass,* p. 15.

[7] *Epistola ad Philadelphienses,* IV—*MPG,* V, 700; Fortescue, *ibid.*, p. 14; Husslein, *The Mass,* p. 200; and *Epistola ad Smyrneos,* VIII, 1-2—*MPG,* V, 713; Fortescue, *The Mass,* pp. 14-15; Husslein, *ibid.*, p. 202.

for the formation of the different Rites.[8] Since it is the bishop who rules the Church, and where he is there the Church is also, nothing can be done in the Church without the bishop or without his permission. The Holy Eucharist can be celebrated validly only by the bishop or by one to whom he gives permission to celebrate. Whatever the bishop wishes to be done at the Sacrifice, whatever customs or ceremonies he wants to be observed, these must be carried out by all who celebrate the Holy Eucharist with his permission. Accordingly, in the beginning, it was the bishop who regulated the ceremonies of the Holy Eucharist.[9]

St. Justin the Martyr (100/10-163/7) furnishes much important testimony about the Sacrifice of the Mass in the early days of the Church. In his First Apology addressed to Antoninus Pius (138-161) he defends the Christians against the charges of impiety to the gods and of an immoral life by praising the holiness and piety of the early Christians themselves and of their doctrines and worship. St. Justin also describes the liturgy of Baptism and of the Eucharist. He explains how the Holy Eucharist is celebrated after the administration of the Sacrament of Baptism. The one who has just been baptized is brought to join the other faithful in prayer. After the prayers and the kiss of peace, the Holy Eucharist is celebrated. The bishop and the people give thanks, and the deacons then distribute Holy Communion to all present and carry it to those who are absent.[10]

St. Justin tells us that the Holy Eucharist was celebrated by the bishop—**ὁ προεστώς**, *antistes.* The species offered for consecration were bread and wine mixed with water: «ἄρτος καὶ ποτήριον ὕδατος καὶ κράματος»—"panis et poculum aquae et vini aqua mixti."[11] Quasten in his work explains that "τὸ κρᾶμα est vinum aqua mixtum."[12] He further explains that two chalices were brought to the bishop, one containing water and the other containing wine mixed with water.

[8] *MPG,* V, 713.

[9] Cf. Funk, *A Manual of Church History,* I, 64.

[10] *Apologia I,* c. 65—Quasten, *Monumenta,* I, 16; Fortescue, *The Mass,* p. 18; Husslein, *The Mass,* p. 193; Duchesne, *Christian Worship,* p. 52.

[11] C. 65, 3.

[12] *Monumenta,* I, 16, ftn. 3.

St. Justin describes the Eucharist twice. In chapter 65 he describes the Mass celebrated after the administration of the Sacrament of Baptism. The chalice containing water is given to the newly baptized. This giving of the chalice of water to the newly baptized was to symbolize the cleansing of the inner man.

In chapter 67 St. Justin describes the Mass celebrated on Sunday— «καὶ τῇ τοῦ ἡλίου λεγομένῃ ἡμέρᾳ» —"et die qui dicitur solis" —saying that bread and wine mixed with water are brought to the bishop, who consecrates both species. Both chapters refer to the same Eucharistic rite, except that in the baptismal Eucharist the Baptismal ceremony takes the place of the liturgy of the catechumens.

In both chapters, also, St. Justin mentions that all present receive Holy Communion in both forms from the deacons, who also carry the Sacred Species to those not present.

In chapter 66, n. 1, this spiritual food, the consecrated bread and wine, is called by its technical name "Eucharist"— «εὐχαριστία». In number 3 of the same chapter, St. Justin also includes the words of consecration as used by Our Lord: "Do this in remembrance of me, this is my body; and likewise having taken the chalice and given thanks, he said: this is my blood, and gave only to them [His Apostles]." [13]

After the testimony of St. Justin, such clear and detailed descriptions of the Holy Eucharist are not found in the writings of the Fathers of the third century. The reason for this reticence was the growing practice of the *disciplina arcani* [14] and the development of the different Rites. Fortescue (1874-1923) states that instead of the uniformity (at least in the main lines) of the service in the earliest period, in the third century there already became noticeable the traces of the divergent practices in different countries which eventually brought about the various liturgies.[15] Already in the

[13] Quasten, *Monumenta*, I, 18; Fortescue, *The Mass*, p. 19; Husslein, *The Mass*, p. 229.

[14] A practice of the ancient Church by which knowledge of the more sacred portions of the Holy Eucharist were kept from the unbaptized. It was a custom intended to shield the doctrines and mysteries of Christianity from ridicule or misconception.—King, *Notes on the Catholic Liturgies*, p. 14.

[15] *Ibid.*, p. 28. The uniformity was in outline, not in detail; it was a uni-

third century different localities had injected their customs and their language into the Eucharistic Sacrifice, so that the original uniformity was disappearing. Still, a coherent local liturgy was forming in these different places and, instead of reflecting a uniformity that was universal, it gave evidence of a local uniformity. However, for the period of the development of these local liturgies preceding the date at which they appeared more clearly distinct one can glean interesting information regarding the development of the ceremonies of the Mass and of the administration of Holy Communion from the writings of the second and third centuries.

In the year 1830, seven fragments of an old epitaph carved in Greek characters on stone were found in an old cemetery at Autun in France. This was the *Epitaphium Pectorii.*[16] In this epitaph of eleven verses, Pectorius treats of Baptism and of the Eucharist, and in the last verses he prays for his parents and brothers who are dead. Because of the *disciplina arcani,* Pectorius uses figurative language. In verses 5 and 6, where he speaks of the Holy Eucharist, an important reference to the manner of distributing Holy Communion in the early years of the Church is given:

> Salvatoris sanctorum mellitum accipe cibum;
> manduca, bibe, piscem tenens manibus.[17]

Those referred to as *sancti* are the baptized Christians. The word *piscem* is figuratively used by the early Christians to signify

formity still subject to change in its details. It was the insistence on one detail in one place, on another somewhere else, the enlarging or shortening of different parts in the different churches, which led to the evolution of the various Liturgies or Rites in the Church. Cf. Fortescue, *ibid.*, pp. 47-53.

[16] According to Cardinal Pitra (1812-1889), who first edited the *Epitaphium Pectorii,* and G. B. DeRossi (1822-1894), the epitaph dates back to the second century. Fathers Lenormant (1802-1859), LeBlant (1818-1897) and J. Wilpert (1857-1944) thought that it went back to the end of the third century; still others place the time as the fourth century, 350-400 A. D., in view of the form of the Greek letters used. But the author, Pectorius, uses the same symbolic words which were known as early as the second century.—Quasten, *Monumenta,* I, 24.

[17] Σωτῆρος ἁγίων μελινδέα λάμβανε βρῶσιν;
Ἔσθιε πινάων ἰχθὺν ἔχων παλάμαις.
—Quasten, *Monumenta*, I, 26-27.

Christ. The walls of the catacombs are full of pictures of fish, and reveal the frequent use of the Greek word ἰχθύς. Therefore, "holding the fish in the hands" means that the Christians received the Body of Christ in their hands at Communion and then communicated themselves. The words *manduca* and *bibe* signify that Communion was distributed under both forms.

St. Irenaeus (c. 140-202) likewise mentions the matter of the Holy Eucharist as being bread and wine.[18] St. Irenaeus bears witness to the practice of sending the Holy Eucharist to people who are absent, in this case to other bishops as a sign of peace and intercommunion, in his letter to Pope St. Victor I (189-198) at the time of the Paschal controversy. He wrote this letter in the name of the Church of Gaul, beseeching the Pope to reconsider his decree of excommunication against Polycrates, Bishop of Ephesus, and the Churches of Asia Minor who held that Easter should be celebrated on the fourteenth of Nisan. He tells the Pope that his predecessors did not observe the fourteenth of Nisan, but nevertheless any strangers in Rome who did observe that day were never cast out because of it, but they could observe it in peace. And the priests of Rome, though they did not observe the fourteenth of Nisan, sent the Holy Eucharist to those who did observe that day, thus signifying their friendship. St. Irenaeus further remarks that when St. Polycarp (d. 155/156) visited Pope Anicetus (ca. 154-165) in Rome, they disagreed on the question. But Pope Anicetus nevertheless as a mark of respect allowed Polycarp to administer the Eucharist.[19]

The Fathers of the third century, writing when the *disciplina arcani* was in force, repeat the testimony of the early Fathers with regard to the Holy Eucharist and Holy Communion. They add their authority to the testimony already given. The matter of the

[18] *Adversus Haereses,* lib. IV, c. 18, nn. 4-5—*MPG,* VII, 1027; Fortescue, *The Mass,* p. 27; Husslein, *The Mass,* p. 239; cf. also pp. 233-241.

[19] Eusebius, *Historia Ecclesiastica,* lib. V, cc. 23-24—*Die griechischen christlichen Schriftsteller der ersten drei Jahrhunderte* (7 vols. in 10), II, Pars I (*Eusebius Werke,* ed. Schwartz, Leipzig, 1903), 489-497 (hereafter cited *GCS*); Eusebius, *Church History* (2 vols., New York, 1890), Vol. I, lib. V, cc. 23-24, pp. 241-244. Fortescue, *The Mass,* p. 27. James Meagher, *The Seven Gates of Heaven* (7. ed., New York, 1892), p. 198.

Holy Eucharist is bread and wine mixed with water.[20] In connection with the Holy Sacrifice the people received Holy Communion in both species.[21] They also received standing,[22] and the celebrant distributed the Body of Our Lord into their outstretched hands,[23] while the deacon administered the consecrated chalice after him.[24]

The reception of Holy Communion in both species was the ordinary custom. However, Communion under one form only was also known. It was clearly understood by the early Christians that to receive Holy Communion in only one form satisfied the command of Christ to eat His Flesh and drink His Blood.

To attend Mass and not to receive Holy Communion was unthinkable among the early Christians. However, since Mass was not said every day in the early days of the Church, the Christians nevertheless desired to communicate more frequently. To satisfy this desire, they were permitted to take home with them part of the consecrated bread which they received at Mass. Tertullian gives evidence of this custom in a letter to his wife in which he explains to her the disadvantage of a Christian woman marrying a pagan.[25] Besides bearing witness to the reception of Holy Communion at home and in one kind, this letter of Tertullian implies also that Holy Communion was received fasting and that the bread used may

[20] St. Cyprian (cc. 200-258), *Epistula LXIII (ad Caecilium)*, c. 13—*MPL*, IV, 383; (cf. also cc. 2, 5, 9, 10, 11—*MPL*, IV, 374-382); Fortescue, *ibid.*, p. 42; St. Hippolytus (d. 235), *Traditio Apostolica*—Quasten, *Monumenta*, I, 32-33.

[21] Origen (185/6-254/5), *Commentarium in Evangelium secundum Joannem, Tomus XXVIII*, c. 4—*MPG*, XIV, 687; Fortescue, *ibid.*, p. 32; St. Cyprian, *De Lapsis*, c. 25—*MPL*, IV, 485; Fortescue, *ibid.*, p. 43; Husslein, *The Mass*, pp. 252-255; Dom Jean de Puniet, *The Mass: Its Origin and History* (New York: Longmans, Green & Co., 1930), p. 189.

[22] Tertullian (ca. 160-ca. 240), *De Oratione*, c. 19—*MPL*, I, 1181; St. Cyprian, *ibid.*, c. 22—*MPL*, IV, 483; Dionysius of Alexandria (d. 264/5), *Epistola IV ad Sixtum II*—*MPL*, V, 97A; Eusebius, *Historia Ecclesiastica*, lib. VII, c. 9—*GCS*, Vol. II, pars 2 (1908), 649. Fortescue, *The Mass*, p. 34.

[23] Tertullian, *De Spectaculis*, c. 25—*CSEL*, XX, 25; *MPL*, I, 657; *Liber de Idolatria*, c. 7—*CSEL*, XX, 37; *MPL*, I, 669. Cf. *De Corona*, c. 2—*MPL*, II, 80; Fortescue, *ibid.*, p. 32; Dionysius of Alexandria, *loc. cit.*

[24] Tertullian, *De Corona*, *loc. cit.*; St. Cyprian, *De Lapsis*, *loc. cit.*

[25] *Ad Uxorem*, lib. II, c. 5—*MPL*, I, 1296. Cf. Origen, *In Exodum XIII*, c. 3—*MPG*, XII, 391.

well have been fermented bread—the kind of bread in common use.[26]

Dionysius of Alexandria (248-264/5) in writing a letter to Pope Fabius (236-250) tells of the administering of Holy Communion in one kind in the form of Viaticum. A dying man, Serapion by name, sent his nephew for the priest that he might receive the last Sacraments. The priest himself being sick could not come. Accordingly, the priest gave the boy a small portion of the Holy Eucharist and told him to soak it and let the drops fall into the man's mouth. It seems more probable that the boy soaked the Holy Eucharist in water, and not in wine; certainly not in consecrated wine.[27]

This testimony, then, offers clues to the customs underlying the development in the celebration of the Mass and in the administration of Holy Communion in the first three centuries up to the I Council of Nicaea in 325. This Council itself issued two canons which pertain to the distribution of Holy Communion and Holy Viaticum. It has already been stated that the celebrant distributed the Body of Our Lord, while the deacon followed him with the chalice containing the Precious Blood. There had grown up a custom whereby in some cities the deacon communicated priests and even partook of the Holy Eucharist before the bishop. The Council reprobated this custom in no uncertain terms and commanded the deacons to remain in their own sphere—they were ministers to the bishop and also inferior to the priests.[28]

With regard to Holy Viaticum, the Council of Nicaea legislated that no dying person was to be deprived of the last and necessary Viaticum. Therefore the bishop was to share this great gift with anyone of the faithful who was dying and who asked to receive Holy Communion. Such a one was also to be remembered in the prayers of all.[29]

[26] *Loc. cit.*: "Non sciet maritus, quid secreto ante omnem cibum gustes; et si sciverit panem, non illum credit esse qui dicitur?"

[27] Eusebius, *Historia Ecclesiastica*, lib. VI, c. 44—*GCS*, II, pars 2, 625.

[28] I Council of Nicaea (325), can. 18—Mansi, II, 675; Hardouin, I, 331.

[29] Canon 13—Fonti, *Codificazione Canonica Orientale* (XVI Fascicoli, Romae: Tipografia Poliglotta Vaticana, 1930-1937), Fascicolo IX, *Disciplina Generalis*, n. 868 (hereafter cited *Fonti*). Cf. Pitra, *Iuris Ecclesiastici Graecorum Historia et Monumenta* (2 vols., Romae: 1864), I, 432 (hereafter cited Pitra, *Historia et Monumenta*) and also Meagher, *The Seven Gates of Heaven*, p. 205.

## CHAPTER III

### SUMMARY

THE sources of the first three centuries reveal in regard to the ceremonies of the celebration of Mass and the administration of Holy Communion the following elements of general observance. The celebration of the Holy Sacrifice was called the Eucharist. The matter to be consecrated was bread and wine mixed with water. The bread was broken. Holy Communion was distributed in both forms—the Body of Christ by the priest, the Precious Blood by the deacon. Only the baptized could receive, and the faithful usually made their confession before receiving Holy Communion. The people stood when receiving, and the priest placed the Body of Our Lord into their hands; they drank from the consecrated chalice held by the deacon. Holy Communion was carried by the deacon to those who were not present. The custom was to receive every time one attended the Holy Sacrifice, but Holy Communion in one form—under the species of bread—was sometimes taken home, there to be received by the people before they broke their fast. Holy Viaticum was given under one form also—that of bread.

# PART II

# FROM THE I COUNCIL OF NICAEA (325) TO THE COUNCIL OF TRENT (1545-1563)

## CHAPTER I

## THE ORIGIN OF RITES

THE term "Rite" can be taken in a broad sense or in a strict sense. In the broad meaning of the term, the word "Rite" comprises in its concept every part of the discipline established by the Church and as introduced either through use or custom approved by the Church. Therefore the term "Rite" in the broad sense points to all the laws and customs which determine the hierarchical constitution of the Church and which regulate the government of the Church.

In the strict sense the word "Rite" is used to denote the liturgy, and then it designates the positive and precise regulating of public worship. "Rite," in this sense, includes every legitimate expression of public worship, that is, every form authorized by the command of God or by the precept of the Church, of externally performing the sacred functions.[1]

From the fourth century onward the liturgical freedom previously allowed to every celebrant to extemporize the Eucharistic prayers, with the exception of the words of Consecration, disappeared. Instead, a stabilized and fixed form of liturgy came into being. In different places, however, there were different liturgies, although all could be traced back to a common root. The reason for the different liturgies is the reason for the different Rites, taken in the strict sense.

That reason was the following that in various places, varying

[1] Gommarus Michiels, O.M.C., *Normae Generales Juris Canonici* (2 vols., Lublin-Polonia: Universitas Catholica, 1929), I, 38, 48 (hereafter cited *Normae*).

customs and ideas led to the insistence on one part of the liturgy rather than on another; different parts with their prayers were lengthened or shortened, or their order was rearranged; more elaborate and imposing ceremonies were used in some parts than in others. The customs of the larger cities were imitated in the neighboring towns, and dependent dioceses naturally followed their Patriarchal city.

The three outstanding Rites were those which originated in the Patriarchal cities of Rome, Antioch and Alexandria. These three Rites are called the parent Rites. To these must be added the Rite which originated in Gaul. Duchesne (1843-1922) enumerates the four parent Rites—two in the East: Syrian and Alexandrian; and two in the West: Roman and Gallican. He suggests that these four Rites might be reduced to two, a division analogous to that which obtains today, namely, the Roman and the Antiochene or Syrian as used in Constantinople, since these two have almost absorbed the rest.[2]

The reason for the importance of Rome, of Antioch and of Alexandria is known; they were the Patriarchical cities.[3] The orgin of the Gallican Rite is not certain, although Duchesne thinks it not impossible to trace the Gallican back to the Syrian Rite. Quasten, analyzing the liturgy of the Gallican Mass, gives evidence of the strong influence of the Oriental liturgies on the Gallican Liturgy. His analysis shows that while the influence of the Oriental liturgies was exceptionally strong, the Gallican Liturgy was nevertheless manifold in origin and not traceable to any one Oriental liturgy. It does appear, however, that the Syriac liturgies exercised the greatest influence on the Liturgy of Gaul.[4]

The Byzantine Rite is derived from the Antiochene. St. Basil the Great, Archbishop of Caesarea in Cappadocia (370-379), ar-

[2] *Christian Worship*, p. 55.

[3] The I Council of Nicaea (325) stated in canon 6 that Alexandria and Antioch were constituted as Patriarchates similar to the Patriarchate of Rome, but nevertheless subordinate to Rome.—Hardouin, I, 326.

[4] Johannes Quasten, "Oriental Influence in the Gallican Liturgy,"—*Traditio* (New York: Cosmopolitan Science and Art Service Co., Inc., edited by Johannes Quasten and Stephen Kuttner, 1943), I, 55-78. Cf. King, *Notes on the Catholic Liturgies*, pp. 111, 253; Fortescue, *The Mass*, p. 100.

ranged the liturgy of his Church. He shortened it somewhat, and in this form the Rite spread to Constantinople. There it became the origin of the Great Byzantine Liturgy. St. John Chrysostom, Archbishop of Constantinople (398-407), again reformed and shortened the Liturgy of St. Basil, and this Liturgy of St. John Chrysostom is the one commonly used in the Byzantine Rite, as St. Nicephorus (806-815) tells us:

> "Agnoscendum quomodo Nicephorus et Tarasius, decantati patriarchae, cum reliqua synodo sancta in certo ordine liturgias composuerunt, communem vero semper esse quae Chrysostomi est."[5]

The older form, the Liturgy of St. Basil, is retained by the Byzantine Rite for a few days in the year: the feast of the Exaltation of the Holy Cross (September 14), Christmas Eve, the feast of St. Basil (January 1), the Eve of the feast of the Epiphany, the Sundays throughout the greater Lent (except Palm Sunday), Holy Thursday and Holy Saturday.[6]

A third Liturgy, attributed to Pope St. Gregory the Great (590-604), is also used by the Byzantine Rite. This is the *Liturgy of the Presanctified.* It is used on each weekday in Lent, except Saturday. The Trullan Synod (692) stated the days on which this Liturgy was to be celebrated:

> "In omnibus sanctae quadragesimae jejunii diebus, praeterquam sabbato et dominica et sancto Annunciationis die, fiat sacra Praesanctificatorum liturgia."[7]

[5] *Fonti,* IX, n. 566; Pitra, *Historia et Monumenta,* II, 320-321.

[6] St. Nicephorus: "Magni vero Basilii liturgiam alteram undecim reservari diebus, quae quidem sunt: XIV septembris in exaltatione venerandae et salvificae crucis, in qua quisque christiano nomine dictum Dei populus jejunium perficit; in vigilia nativitatis Christi, in memora edicti ejusdem patris ad januarii primam diem, similiter in vigilia luminum, in dominicis magnae quadragesimae, exclusa palmarum die, in sancta et magna feria V, in sancto majore sabbato, extra praefatos dies, Basilii magni liturgia in sacris non usurpatur."—*Fonti,* IX, 565; Pitra, *op. cit.,* II, 321. The "greater Lent" *(magna quadragesima)* is that Lent which precedes Easter.

[7] Canon 52—*Fonti,* IX, n. 608; Pitra, *ibid.,* p. 51.

St. Nicephorus also defined when the Liturgy of the Presanctified was to be used, and he called it the work of Pope Gregory the Great. He prescribed that the Liturgy of the Presanctified was to be used three times a week, and this superseded the provision of the Trullan Synod.[8]

These three Liturgies are still in use today by both the Catholic and Dissident Orientals. In the Latin Church, the Mass of the Presanctified is now said only on Good Friday, but it was once used more frequently throughout the year.[9]

Special mention was made of the Byzantine Rite because that Rite is the one in most common use among the Orientals, and in this work comparison will be for the most part between the Latin Rite and the Byzantine Rite.

[8] "De liturgia vero praesanctificatorum, quae opera est Gregorii reverendissimi nostri patris Papae Romani, cui nomen Dialogus est, ter fieri in singulis sanctae quadragesimae septimanis definimus."—*Fonti,* IX, n. 609; Pitra, *ibid.*, p. 321.

[9] Fortescue, *The Orthodox Eastern Church* (London: Catholic Truth Society, 1907), p. 412, ftn. 2.

## CHAPTER II

## THE NAME OF THE EUCHARISTIC SACRIFICE

In connection with the diversity of Rites, it is indicated also to mention the difference in name as applied to the celebration of the Eucharistic Sacrifice by the Western and the Eastern Church. Many names had been given to the celebration of the Holy Sacrifice throughout the centuries before it acquired a technical name. One of the first names was the *Breaking of Bread.*[1] Another early name was the *Lord's Supper.*[2] The name *Eucharist* came into use rather early too. The *Didache* uses this term when referring to the Holy Sacrifice, and it is probable that the term is used in a technical sense.[3] St. Justin (100/10-163/7) at any rate uses the term *Eucharist* in a technical sense, and with it designates the Divine Sacrifice.[4]

In the Western Church, the name *Missa* (Mass) is applied to all the rites and ceremonies, words and actions, by which the Eucharistic Sacrifice is offered. The term "Mass" comes from the Latin *missio,* which meant *dismissal. Missio* was commonly used for a dismissal of any kind, but gradually it came to be exclusively used in the Eucharistic service. At first the term was used solely to designate the dismissal of the catechumens, but later it was used to denote the dismissal of the faithful as well. The first occurrence of the term "Mass" as applied to the liturgy of the faithful is found in a letter of St. Ambrose (d. 397).[5]

Florus of Lyons (d. 860) explains the word thus:

> "Missa nihil aliud intelligitur quam dimissio. . . . Missa ergo catechumenorum fiebat ante actionem sacramenti; missa fidelium fit post confectionem et participationem." [6]

[1] Acts, ii, 42, 46; xx, 7.

[2] 1 Cor., xi, 20.

[3] C. IX, n. 1—Quasten, *Monumenta,* I, p. 10.

[4] *Apologia I,* c. 66, 1—Quasten, *ibid.,* p. 17.

[5] *Epistola I,* 20, nn. 4-5—*MPL,* XVI, 995. Cf. Fortescue, *The Mass,* p. 399; King, *Notes on the Catholic Liturgies,* p. 55; Attwater, *The Catholic Eastern Churches,* p. 32.

[6] *De Actione Missae,* n. 92—*MPL,* CXIX, 72.

There were, then, two *missae* spoken of, one of the catechumens, the other of the faithful. After the Catechumenate disappeared, the word *missa* referred to the whole Eucharistic sacrifice.

The word "Mass" signifies not only the sacrifice, which derives from the divine law, but also the rites and ceremonies, which derive from the ecclesiastical law.[7]

The Orientals do not in their own language call the Eucharistic Sacrifice the Mass. Therefore, to speak of the Oriental Liturgy as the Mass would be inaccurate. What the Western Church calls the Mass, the Oriental Church calls the "Holy Liturgy," or simply the "Liturgy." In the beginning, liturgy (λειτουργία) meant any public service in the Church. From this meaning the term became restricted to designate the most important service, namely, the celebration of the Eucharistic Sacrifice. This use of the term "Liturgy" is retained in the Oriental Church to signify exactly what the Latin term *Missa* signifies, that is, the celebration of the Holy Sacrifice and the ordinary manner of that celebration. Distinct from it is the manner of performing the sacred rites in other functions, for example, in the divine office or in the administration of the Sacraments and the Sacramentals.[8]

The Eastern name "Liturgy," however, is older than the Western name "Mass," although both designate the same act of worship, the Eucharistic Sacrifice.

[7] The word "Rite" is more comprehensive in meaning than the term "ceremonies." Ceremonies are included within the meaning of Rite and are a part of it. They are the exterior forms of divine worship, things or actions, prescribed by the Church symbolically to signify something spiritual, either naturally or by the intention of the Church.—Michiels, *Normae,* I, 48. Cf. also the Council of Trent, sess. XXII, cap. 5; Petrus Gasparri, *Tractatus Canonicus de Sanctissima Eucharistia* (2 vols., Parisiis, 1897), II, p. 162, n. 853 (hereafter cited *De Eucharistia*).

[8] F. X. Wernz, *Ius Decretalium* (6 vols., Romae et Prati, 1898-1905), III, pars 2, n. 314.

## CHAPTER III

## LANGUAGE

In the first centuries the Holy Sacrifice was celebrated in the vernacular of the people. The people recited the prayers with the celebrant in the spoken language of their day, and the bishop or priest preached in the tongue spoken in his locality. After the ceremonies used in celebrating the Holy Sacrifice had become more nearly fixed, the language also was made uniform in order that the form of the Mass would not be subject to change. Sacramentaries, prayer-books and hymn-books were written for this purpose.

In the period up to the third century the liturgical language of Rome was not Latin but Greek. The Fathers and writers of the first two centuries wrote in Greek, the inscriptions in the catacombs were in Greek, and the Sacred Scriptures that were used were in Greek.

> "Greek," says King, "appears to have been a divine plan for the use of the Christian Church and the spread of the Gospel in primitive times. A Hellenistic dialect, found in Alexandria after the wars of Alexander the Great, and providing the texts of the Septuagint version of the Bible as well as of the earliest liturgies, was used." [1]

Just when Latin finally displaced Greek in the Roman Church is not certain, but the change was not a sudden one. Latin gradually began to supersede Greek as the ecclesiastical language in Rome. For a time both languages were used more or less indiscriminately. It was, for instance, the custom at one time to read the Epistle, the Prophecies, and the Gospel in both languages.

Thomassinus (1619-1695) relates that the custom of using both languages prevailed even in the ninth century, so that in Solemn Masses at Rome the Epistle and Gospel were chanted first in Greek and then in Latin, while at Constantinople they were sung first in

[1] King, *Notes on the Catholic Liturgies*, pp. 329-331.

Latin and then in Greek. The reason for this was the intent to show more clearly the unity of the two Churches.[2]

This custom remains today when the Holy Father solemnly celebrates Mass. The Epistle is first chanted in Latin by a Latin subdeacon, then in Greek by a Greek subdeacon; the Gospel is also sung in Latin by a Latin deacon, then in Greek by a Greek deacon.[3] This practice at a solemn Papal Mass of chanting the Epistle and the Gospel in Greek as well as in Latin dates from a time before the schism of Michael Cerularius in 1053.[4]

The Council of Trent legislated that the vernacular language was not to be used in the celebration of Mass:

> "Etsi Missa magnam contineat populi fidelis eruditionem, non tamen expedire visus est Patribus, ut vulgari passim lingua celebraretur." [5]

And in canon 9 of its twenty-second session, the Council condemned anyone for saying that the vernacular language alone should be used in the celebrating of Mass:

> "Si quis dixerit . . . lingua tantum vulgari Missam celebrari debere . . . A. S." [6]

The language used by the Orientals is not as definitely fixed as it is in the Latin Rite. Among them also the language in the beginning was the vernacular of the local faithful, e. g., Aramaic at first in Jerusalem, Greek at Antioch and Alexandria. However, the difference was that among the Orientals the practice continued of using the national language of the peoples among whom the Rite

[2] Ludovicus Thomassinus, *Vetus et Nova Ecclesiae Disciplina circa Beneficia et Beneficiarios* (10 vols., Magontiaci, 1787), pars I, lib. II, cap. 82, n. 3. Cf. King, *ibid.*, 364-365.

[3] Gasparri, *De Eucharistia*, II, p. 160, n. 851.

[4] King, *loc. cit.*

[5] Sess. XXII, *de sacrificio Missae*, c. 8—Denzinger-Bannwart-Umberg, *Enchiridion Symbolorum Definitionum et Declarationum de Rebus Fidei et Morum* (ed. 21-23, St. Louis: Herder & Co., 1937), n. 946 (hereafter cited Denzinger, *Enchiridion*).

[6] Denzinger, *Enchiridion*, n. 956.

was introduced so that besides the Greek language the Slavic,[7] Roumanian, Arabic, Syriac, Armenian and Coptic languages were used by the respective peoples in the celebration of the Holy Liturgy.[8] The Syriac language is no longer used to celebrate the Liturgy of the Byzantine Rite, and Georgian is now only used by one Catholic Georgian congregation at Constantinople.[9]

The language of the Liturgy is one point on which there is still no attempt by the Orientals at uniformity. In most cases the liturgical language in the vernacular tongue as first used by the respective peoples was retained even though throughout the years the vernacular itself changed. The Greek, for example, which the Greeks and the Italo-Greeks use to chant the Byzantine Liturgy is much different from the Greek now used by the people.[10]

Other languages are used by smaller communities of the "Orthodox" Eastern Church in celebrating the Byzantine Liturgy. These languages are: German, Esthonian and Lettish in the the Baltic provinces; Finnish and Tartar in Finland and Siberia; Eskimo and North American Indian in Alaska; Chinese and Japanese. One congregation by Lake Egerdir in Asia Minor uses Turkish.[11] In the United States there are eleven dissident Oriental sects listed under the general heading of Eastern Orthodox Churches. Eight of these sects, namely, the Albanian, Bulgarian, Greek, Roumanian, Russian, Serbian, Syrian and Ukrainian, use their native language when performing the Liturgy. The remaining three, namely, the American

[7] The Staro-Slav (Old Slav) language, used liturgically by most of the Slav races, dates from the days of the Apostles Saints Cyril (d. 869) and Methodius (d. 885), and was confirmed by Pope John VIII (872-882), who authorized Slavonic in perpetuity for all the divine offices of the Church.—Jaffé, n. 3268. Cf. King, *Notes on the Catholic Liturgies*, p. 371; Nicholas Gihr, *The Holy Sacrifice of the Mass* (12. ed., St. Louis: B. Herder Book Co., 1937), p. 319, ftn. 2.

[8] Joseph Papp-Szilagyi: "Proprium est Ecclesiae Orientalis ut in sacris lingua nationali utatur; ita praeter linguam graecam, lingua slavica, romanica, arabica, syriaca, armenica et coptica in sacris apud respectivos populos adhibetur et etiam sacra liturgia celebratur."—*Enchiridion Juris Ecclesiae Orientalis Catholicae* (2. ed., Magna-Varadini, 1880), pars II, n. 52.

[9] Fortescue, *The Mass*, p. 92.

[10] King, *ibid.*, pp. 329-331.

[11] Cf. Fortescue, *The Orthodox Eastern Church*, p. 397. Cf. also Fortescue, *The Mass*, p. 92; Salaville, *Eastern Liturgies*, pp. 31-51.

Holy Orthodox Catholic Eastern Church, the Apostolic Episcopal Church (the Holy Eastern Catholic and Apostolic Orthodox Church) and the Holy Orthodox Church in America, use English.[12]

[12] *Religious Bodies, 1936,* Statistics, History, Doctrine, Organization and Work, U. S. Department of Commerce, Bureau of the Census (2 vols., United States Government Printing Office: Washington, D. C., 1941), II, 549.

# CHAPTER IV

## THE *ANTIMENSION*

THE holy table on which the unbloody Sacrifice of the Cross is offered to God is called by all Christians the altar. In the first days of the Church Mass was celebrated on wooden altars. The reasons for this practice were that the Apostles and their successors wanted to imitate Christ who offered Himself in the Eucharist while still at the table of the Paschal Supper. Therefore they too used a wooden altar to celebrate the Lord's Supper. Since the Apostles were engaged in spreading the Faith of Christ, they traveled from place to place and preached to the different peoples. It is very probable, then, that they celebrated Mass most of the time on a wooden altar, because it would have been practically impossible to find a stone or marble altar. Even if there were stone altars in some pagan communities,[1] the Apostles would never even have entertained the idea of offering the Holy Sacrifice on pagan altars. Likewise, during the time of the persecutions it hardly would have been wise to construct permanent altars that would most likely have been destroyed.

After the persecutions, when the Church had gained her freedom, some churches retained the wooden altars, and some even used altars made of metal—gold or silver.[2] But altars likewise came to be made of stone, as is evident from those found in the catacombs. Gradually it became the custom to have all altars made of stone, since these were more durable, not subject to decay like wood, or to corrosion like common metals, and also less expensive than precious

[1] Acts, xvii, 23.

[2] Cardinal Bona (1609-1674) mentions that Constantine the Great (306-337) erected seven altars of most pure silver in the Basilica of Constantinople. Each altar weighed 260 pounds. And Pope Sixtus III (432-440) is said to have presented an altar of the purest silver, weighing 300 pounds, to the Basilica of Saint Mary.—*Rerum Liturgicarum Libri Duo* (Romae: 1671), lib. I, cap. XX, n. 1, p. 149 (hereafter cited *Res Liturgicae*).

altars.[3] The custom of having stone altars became law in the Council of Epaône in southeastern France (517).[4] Canon 26 of this Council states:

"Altaria si non fuerint lapidea, chrismatis non consecrentur." [5]

In the case of the Orientals who were under the domination of the Mohammedans, it was difficult for them to have stationary and permanent altars. The Mohammedans often invaded the churches, threw everything out, profaned the altars, and then converted the church into a temple of their own.[6]

The custom for these Christians for many centuries was to have only the table or *mensa* on which were placed the white cloths consecrated by the bishop, or else they had only a thin piece of marble, such as is now called a portable altar. The reason for this was that, if the Mohammedans disturbed the celebration of the Liturgy, the cloths or the altar-stone could be easily picked up and removed before the Infidels could desecrate them. The stones as altars, as well as the table and the white cloths, were consecrated with chrism by the bishop, and no one could celebrate the Liturgy except on the consecrated cloths or on a consecrated altar-stone.[7]

The use of the *Antimension* ('Αντιμίνσια) by the Orientals dates from this time also, and for the same reasons. The *Antimension* corresponds to the Latin corporal and altar-stone. It is a square piece of linen doubled, in which are sewn relics anointed with chrism by the bishop. The *Antimension* is always consecrated by an Oriental bishop. Ordinarily it is about 10 inches wide and 14

[3] Cf. Ayrinhac, *Administrative Legislation in the New Code of Canon Law* (New York: Longmans, Green & Co., 1930), p. 48, n. 41 (hereafter cited *Administrative Legislation*); Augustine, *A Commentary on the New Code of Canon Law* (8 vols., St. Louis: B. Herder Book Co.), Vol. VI (3. ed., 1931), 85.

[4] Van Hove (*Commentarium Lovaniense in Codicem Iuris Canonici*, Vol. I, Tom. I, *Prolegomena* [2. ed., Mechliniae-Romae: H. Dessain, 1945], p. 181) identifies Epaône with Albon near Vienne.

[5] C. 31, D. I, *de cons.*

[6] An outstanding example of this is the Church of the Holy Wisdom (Saint Sophia) in Constantinople.

[7] Eusebius Renaudot, *Liturgiarum Orientalium Collectio* (2. ed., 2 vols., London, 1847), I, 164-165 (hereafter cited Renaudot).

inches long and it is richly decorated with religious images and inscriptions.[8] The invasion of the Mohammedans into the churches happened so frequently, as has already been noted, that the bishops were forced to find some way to escape them more easily with the sacred species. The *Antimension* was the answer. The bishops could just fold the *Antimension* over the Body of Christ and escape with the Blessed Sacrament that way.[9]

Cardinal Bona (1609-1674) stated that the *Antimension* was used in the Oriental Church also when the Liturgy was celebrated on an altar that was not consecrated. He cited Manuel Charitopulus [10] as saying that the *Antimension* was not used on all altars, but was placed only on those of which it is not known whether they were consecrated.[11] Although it is true that, if a priest of the Oriental Rite has no consecrated altar, the *Antimension* is sufficient for the celebration of the Liturgy, nevertheless, the *Antimension* must be used even when the altar is consecrated.[12]

St. Nicephorus, Patriarch of Constantinople (806-815), legislated regarding both the necessity and the use of the *Antimension.* He stated that the use of the *Antimension* was so necessary that, if a priest should perform the Liturgy without it, he could be made to perform a penance of one year, and also one hundred acts of penitence (*centum Metanoeae*).[13] The use of the *Antimension* was not lim-

[8] Renaudot, *loc. cit.*; Duskie, *The Canonical Status of the Orientals in the United States,* The Catholic University of America Canon Law Studies, n. 48 (Washington, D. C.: The Catholic University of America, 1928), p. 116; Jacobus Goar, *Euchologion sive Rituale Graecorum Complectens Ritus et Ordines* (Parisiis, 1647), pp. 653-654. See also page 648 for the formula of consecration. Fortescue, *The Orthodox Eastern Church,* p. 409. Fortescue says that he has seen an *Antimension* made of silk also. King, *Notes on the Catholic Liturgies,* p. 401. King also mentions that wooden *Antimensia* were known to both Syrians and Byzantines.

[9] Renaudot, I, 311.

[10] The work *Ius Orientale,* lib. III, is indicated by Cardinal Bona. It is not available for consultation by the present writer.

[11] *Res Liturgicae,* pp. 150-151.

[12] Renaudot, *loc. cit.*; Nicolaus Nilles, *Symbolae ad Illustrandam Historiam Ecclesiae Orientalis in Terris Coronae S. Stephani* (2 vols., Oeniponte, 1885), II, 861, ftn. 1 (hereafter cited *Symbolae*).

[13] Canon 98: "Sacerdos, si liturgiam fecerit sine antimensio, obnoxius est

ited to a particular region, but the *Antimension* was sent to priests of the Oriental Rites who needed it anywhere, and it had to be taken along by a priest if he traveled to another province, just as the holy oils were carried by him. The *Antimension*, however, was not to be used for the performance of the Liturgy in a private house or on board a ship. Anyone who misused the *Antimension* was to be punished without delay.[14]

poenitentiae unius anni et centum Metanoearum."—*Fonti*, IX, n. 15; Pitra, *Historia et Monumenta*, II, 337.

[14] *Ex Constitutionibus*, canons 95, 97, 98—*Fonti*, IX, nn. 15, 16, 17. Pitra, *Historia et Monumenta*, II, 336-337.

## CHAPTER V

## THE EUCHARISTIC BREAD

In all the Rites of the Church the matter for the Holy Eucharist is bread and wine. The Latin Church offers and consecrates unleavened bread (*panis azymus*) in the Mass, while most of the Churches of the Oriental Rite use fermented or leavened bread. However, the Armenians, the Maronites, the Chaldeans, the Syro-Malabars and the Italo-Greeks in a few churches in Sicily, in southern Italy, and in places belonging to the monastery of the Mother of God at Grottaferrata are Oriental Rites which use unleavened bread.[1]

It is not the purpose of this work to discuss the question of whether Christ consecrated leavened or unleavened bread at the Last Supper. The Council of Florence (1438-1445), in the *Decretum pro Graecis,* defined it as an article of faith that the Body of Christ is truly consecrated in wheaten bread whether it be leavened or unleavened; and the priests must consecrate the Body of Our Lord in either the one or the other, each one according to the custom of his Church, whether Western or Eastern.[2]

This definition of the Council of Florence was directed against Michael Cerularius, Patriarch of Constantinople (1043-1058), and others who declared that the use of unleavened bread by the Latin Church was invalid, and that therefore the Latin Church lacked the Eucharist.[3] Michael even went so far as to call the Blessed Sacra-

[1] Gasparri, *De Eucharistia,* II, 120, n. 804; Duskie, *The Canonical Status of the Orientals in the United States,* p. 110; Fortescue, *The Mass,* p. 300; Meagher, *The Seven Gates of Heaven,* p. 188.

[2] "Item (definimus), in azymo sive fermentato pane triticeo corpus Christi veraciter confici; sacerdotesque in altero ipsum Domini corpus conficere debere, unumquemque scilicet juxta suae Ecclesiae sive occidentalis, sive orientalis consuetudinem."—Denzinger, *Enchiridion,* n. 692; Mansi, XXXI B, 1666; cf. King, *Notes on the Catholic Liturgies,* p. 351; John Neale, *A History of the Holy Eastern Church* (2 vols., London, 1850), II, 1075.

[3] Gasparri, *ibid.,* n. 803.

ment, as consecrated by the Latin Church in unleavened bread, *dry mud.*[4]

In the *Decretum pro Armenis,* the Council of Florence stated simply that wheaten bread was to be used:

> "Tertium est Eucharistiae sacramentum, cuius materia est panis triticeus, et vinum de vite, cui ante consecrationem aqua modicissima admisceri debet." [5]

There was no mention in this decree of the specific use either of leavened or of unleavened bread, for the Armenians used the unleavened bread, and never denied the validity of its use for the Mass.

Up to the time of Michael Cerularius there was no disagreement between the Eastern and Western Church about the bread for the Holy Eucharist. Photius (810/15-891/98) in his disagreement with Rome raised no objection to the kind of bread used by the Latin Church. The reasons given for this are that both the Eastern Church and the Western Church used leavened bread, or that the Eastern Church did not know about the use of unleavened bread by the Latin Church. But the more probable reason is that in the first centuries both leavened and unleavened bread were commonly used for the consecrating of the Holy Eucharist according as necessity or opportunity of time and place dictated.[6]

It is not definitely known what kind of bread, whether leavened or unleavened, was used by the early Church. There is a tradition, however, regarding the use of unleavened bread, which was firmly accepted in the Middle Ages. It held that until the breaking out of the Ebionite heresy,[7] the Eastern Church as well as the Western Church used unleavened bread for consecration in the Eucharistic Sacrifice. The Ebionites, who held that it was obligatory to obey

[4] Cornelius Will, *Acta et Scripta Quae de Controversiis Ecclesiae Graecae et Latinae Saeculo Undecimo Composita Extant* (Lipsiae et Marpurgi, 1861), pp. 62 and 105 (hereafter cited as *Acta et Scripta*).

[5] Denzinger, *Enchiridion,* n. 698.

[6] Theophilus Spačil, "Doctrina Theologiae Orientis Separati de Sanctissima Eucharistia,"—*Orientalia Christiana* (36 vols., Romae: Pontificium Institutum Orientalium Studiorum, 1923-1934), Vol. XIV (1929), 135.

[7] Cf. Tixeront, *History of Dogmas* (3 vols., St. Louis, 1910), I, 159-170.

both the Old Law and the Gospels, professed to find a symbol of their belief in unleavened bread. The Fathers of the Church, therefore, adopted the use of leavened bread for the Holy Sacrifice to express their abhorrence of the Ebionite doctrines and to show their disagreement with them. When this heresy died out, the Church of Rome returned to the primitive custom of using unleavened bread, while the Eastern Church retained the later practice of consecrating in leavened bread.[8]

The writings of the Fathers of the first three centuries seem to confirm the opinion that during that time both leavened and unleavened bread were used. Some of the Fathers speak of leavened bread, others of unleavened bread, while still others use the commonly employed word ἄρτος to signify bread, whether leavened or unleavened.

Tertullian, in his letter *Ad Uxorem,* implies that the bread used in the consecration of the Eucharist may well have been leavened bread.[9] St. John Chrysostom (d. 407) attacks the use of unleavened bread and calls it impure, but only as used by the Jews who were still following the Pasch of the Old Law.[10] In another place he affirms the use of leavened bread in the Liturgy. He calls the Body of Christ in the Eucharist, *massam et fermentum*— μᾶζαν καὶ ζύμην.[11] St. Epiphanius (d. 403) reproached the Ebionites because they corrupted the mysteries of the Church by using water only for the Eucharist and by celebrating the Liturgy with unleavened bread.[12]

St. Augustine, Bishop of Hippo (d. 430), in one of his sermons remarks that bread is not simply made of one grain of wheat or even of many grains, but that before the wheat becomes bread it must be ground into flour, mixed with water, and after that baked.

[8] Alzog, *Universal Church History* (4 vols., Dublin, 1874), I, 506, in the footnote. Alzog cites as his authority Pope Innocent III (1198-1216), *De Mysteriis Missae,* lib. IV, cap. 4, as quoting Pope Leo IX (1049-1054). Cf. Neale, *A History of the Holy Eastern Church,* II, 1070-1071. Hore, *Eighteen Centuries of the Orthodox Greek Church* (New York, 1899), p. 400.

[9] Lib. II, c. 5—*MPL,* I, 1296.

[10] *In Proditionem Judae, Homilia I,* n. 5—*MPG,* XLIX, 379-380.

[11] *Homilia XV in 1 Cor.,* n. 4—*MPG,* LXI, 125.

[12] *Adversus Haereses Panarium,* lib. I, pars 2, haer. 30, n. 16—*MPG,* XLI, 432.

Only then does it become bread.[13] Bread made thus out of flour and water alone is simply unleavened bread. St. Thomas Aquinas (1227-1274) quotes St. Gregory the Great (590-604), *In Registro,* as saying that the Roman Church offers unleavened bread because Our Lord assumed flesh that was not mixed with anything else; but the Greek Churches offer leavened bread for the reason that the Word of the Father was clothed with flesh after the manner in which flour has leaven added to it.[14] St. Isidore of Seville (d. 636), in his *Epistola ad Redemptum,* defended against the Orientals the use of unleavened bread for Spain and the Roman Church.[15]

St. Anselm of Canterbury (1033-1109) and Pope Gregory VII (1073-1085) also recognized the validity of the Sacrament of the Eucharist when consecrated in leavened bread by the Latins.[16] St. Peter Damian (d. 1072) was of the opinion that the Latin Church at some time used leavened bread in the Mass.[17] This opinion was afterwards reiterated by Pope Innocent III (1198-1216) in his work *De Sacro Altaris Mysterio.*[18]

Among the Oriental writers, Theophylactus (d. after 1092), Bishop of Achrida in Bulgaria (1078-c. 1092) [19] and Nicetas of Nicomedia, as cited by Anselm, Bishop of Havelberg (1129-1155),[20] speak of the use of unleavened bread by the Latin Church.

Venerable Bede (d. 735) in England,[21] Alcuin (d. 804) in

[13] *Sermo 227, Ad Infantes de Sacramento—MPL,* XXXVIII, 1100.

[14] "Romana ecclesia offert azymos panes, propterea quod Dominus sine ulla commixtione suscepit carnem; sed Graecae ecclesiae offerunt fermentatum, pro eo, quod Verbum Patris indutum est carne, sicut fermentum miscetur farinae."—*Summa Theologica* (6 vols., Taurini, 1886), III, q. 74, a. 4, *in corpore.* Cf. Innocent III, *De Sacro Altaris Mysterio,* lib. IV, c. 4—*MPL,* CCXVII, 857. Gregory the Great, *In Dialogis, Dissertatio VI,* c. XLI—*MPG,* XCIV, 404. Pantaleonis, *Tractatus Contra Graecorum Errores—MPG,* CXL, 524.

[15] *Epistola VII,* nn. 3 et 4—*MPL,* LXXXIII, 906.

[16] St. Anselm, *De Azymo et Fermentato,* c. I—*MPL,* CLVIII, 541-542; Pope Gregory VII, *Epistola ad Gregorium Synnadensem—MPL,* CXLVIII, 573.

[17] *Expositio Canonis Missae,* II—*MPL,* CXLV, 881.

[18] Lib. IV, c. 4—*MPL,* CCXVII, 855.

[19] *Allocutio ad Quemdam ex Suis Familiaribus De Iis Quorum Latini Incusantur,* XV—*MPG,* CXXVI, 245.

[20] *Dialogi III,* c. 19—*MPL,* CLXXXVIII, 1239.

[21] *Expositio in Lucam,* lib. VI, c. 22—*MPL,* XCII, 593, 597.

France,[22] Paschasius Radbertus (d. 860) [23] and Rabanus Maurus (d. 856) in Germany,[24] add their authority to the testimony already given that unleavened bread was used to consecrate the Eucharist in the Roman Church.

Some mention should be made of the *fermentum* which was a fragment of the Host consecrated by the Pope at his Mass and which he sent to the suburban bishops and to the parish priests of Rome. They received it, put it into their chalice and consumed it at the Communion of their Mass. Imitating this custom of the Pope, other bishops also sent the *fermentum* to their priests. A letter of Pope Innocent I (401-417) to Decentius, Bishop of Gubbio, makes reference to this *fermentum*. In this letter the Pope says that the *fermentum* is sent on Sunday to the titular churches of Rome, so that the priests and people who cannot come to the Pope's altar to concelebrate or communicate may know that they are not separated from the Pope's communion. This *fermentum* was taken by acolytes to the churches, but it was not taken to rural or to cemetery churches, because the Sacrament should not be carried long distances.[25] Anastasius Bibliothecarius, writing in the ninth century, also mentions the *fermentum* in connection with Pope Melchiades (311-314). He says that the Pope ordered the oblations from the consecration by the bishop to be sent to the churches, and that these oblations were called the *fermentum*.[26]

The use of the *fermentum* by the bishops and priests corresponded to the use of the *Sancta* by the Pope. The *Sancta* were particles of the Holy Eucharist consecrated at a former Mass and reserved till the next Mass, when they were mixed with the precious Blood at the words: *"Pax Domini sit semper vobiscum."* [27] This

[22] *Epistola XV (ad Fratres Lugdunenses)—MPL,* C, 289.

[23] *De Corpore et Sanguine Domini,* c. 20, n. 3—*MPL,* CXX, 1332.

[24] *De Clericorum Institutione,* lib. I, c. 31: "Nec enim in sacramento aliud offerri licet, nisi quod Dominus ipse constituit, et suo exemplo nos facere docuit. . . . Ergo panem infermentatum et vinum mixtum in sacramentum corporis et sanguinis Christi sanctificari oportet."—*MPL,* CVII, 318.

[25] *Epistola XXV (ad Decentium Episcopum Eugubinum),* c. 5—*MPL,* XX, 556-557.

[26] *Historia de Vitis Romarorum Pontificum—MPL,* CXXVII, 1499-1500.

[27] Fortescue, *The Mass,* pp. 174-175, 366; King, *Notes on the Catholic*

ceremony was to emphasize the unity of the Holy Sacrifice throughout the Church and to mark a continuation from one Mass to the next. St. Irenaeus in his letter to Pope St. Victor bears witness to the practice of the Pope in sending the Holy Eucharist to other bishops as a sign of peace and intercommunion.[28]

The *fermentum* was not the same as the *fermentatum*—fermented bread; the name had no reference to the type of bread used. Fortescue says that "the idea seems to have been that this particle of the Holy Eucharist unites the Church as leaven unites bread. So the name would still be used after azymes alone were consecrated." [29] Spačil notes that Cardinal Bona and others regarded the *fermentum* as the Holy Eucharist consecrated either in unleavened or in leavened bread according to the custom of the churches. It was called *fermentum* because it signified mutual charity, and also in order that the divine mystery might be hidden from non-Christians.[30] On the other hand, Spačil holds with Nicholas of Cusa (1401-1464), Baronius (1538-1607) and others that the *fermentum* does not refer to the Holy Eucharist, but to blessed bread—the *pain bénit* of the French rites, or the *antidoron* of the Eastern Church.[31] However, from what has been said concerning the *fermentum*,[32] the opinion that the *fermentum* was the Holy Eucharist seems the better founded view.

The testimony of the Fathers and Ecclesiastical Writers shows that, although leavened bread was sometimes used, unleavened bread was used in the Church for the first nine centuries. There are those who are of the opinion that the custom of using leavened bread pre-

*Liturgies*, p. 50; Gihr, *The Holy Sacrifice of the Mass*, pp. 706-707, and footnote 3, p. 707.

[28] Cited on page 8. Eusebius, *Historia Ecclesiastica*, V, cc. 23-24—*GCS*, II, pars 1, 489-497.

[29] *Ibid.*, p. 369.

[30] "Art. cit.," *Orientalia Christiana*, XIV (1929), 143-144.

[31] The *antidoron* is the bread which was offered for the service of the altar, but which was not required for consecration. This was distributed immediately after the Communion or a little later. The *Constitutiones Apostolorum* (lib. VIII, c. 31) give the rule for the distribution of this bread which was not needed for consecration.—Mansi, I, 578; *MPG*, I, 1127; cf. also King, *Notes on the Catholic Liturgies*, p. 443; Neale, *Translation of the Primitive Liturgies* (London, 1869), p. 125, and footnote.

[32] Cf. p. 30.

vailed, not only in the Eastern Church, but also in the Western Church for the first eight centuries. They further propose the opinion that unleavened bread was an innovation introduced in the interval between Photius and Michael Cerularius, that is, between 886 and 1053.[33]

It is the common opinion that the custom of the Oriental Church was to use leavened bread in celebrating the Liturgy, although there may have been exceptions. The first certain testimony regarding this custom in the Oriental Church occurs in the work of Joannes Grammaticus (sixth century), *De Paschate Disputatio*, in which he defends the use of leavened bread in the Liturgy.[34]

Until the time of Michael Cerularius, the Western Church and the Eastern Church had no disagreement on the kind of bread to be used in the Eucharistic Sacrifice. Nearly all the Eastern Churches used leavened bread, while in the course of the tenth and eleventh centuries the use of unleavened bread was firmly established in the Western Church.[35] However, the earlier testimony which was cited [36] is evidence that unleavened bread was commonly used in the Western Church from the fifth or sixth century.

It was after the accession of Michael Cerularius to the See of Constantinople (Feb. 20, 1043) that the dissension between the Eastern and the Western Church came to a climax, the disagreement on the kind of bread to be used in the Holy Sacrifice being one of the main issues.

[33] Spačil cites Androutsos as saying that the use of unleavened bread by the Roman Church in the first centuries was exceptional, and that this practice was followed only by heretics. Silvester and Malinovsky, according to him, concede the use of unleavened bread by the Armenians and in Spain from the seventh century, in England from the eighth, in Germany from the ninth, and in Italy from the eleventh century. Mesoloras, Dyobouniotes, Androutsos, Makarij and Malinovsky are cited as asserting that the use of fermented bread was universal in the Church in the first centuries, and that the Roman Church introduced something new—the use of unleavened bread—for the Western Church.—Spačil, "Doctrina Theologiae Orientis Separati de Sanctissima Eucharistia,"—*Orientalia Christiana*, XIII (1928), 245.

[34] Spačil, *ibid.*, p. 144, n. 337.

[35] Cf. Alzog, *Universal Church History*, I, 505, and ftn. 1; Neale, *A History of the Holy Eastern Church*, II, 1073.

[36] Cf. pp. 28-30.

The beginning of the controversy is marked by a letter written in 1053 by Leo, Metropolitan of Achrida in Bulgaria, with the agreement of Michael, to John, Bishop of Trani in Apulia. Apulia had been subject to the Byzantine Church since the days of Leo the Isaurian (717-741).[37] The letter, besides advancing other charges, accused the Latin Church for using unleavened bread. This letter was to be communicated to Pope Leo IX (1049-1054). (Cardinal Humbert translated the letter into Latin.) But it was followed by another letter, which completed the arguments against unleavened bread. It was in this later letter that the unleavened bread used in the consecration of the Holy Eucharist was called *dry mud.*[38]

Pope Leo IX refuted in a general way the accusations of Leo of Achrida in a letter to Michael Cerularius.[39] Cardinal Humbert also refuted the accusations in his *Dialogus.* He remarked that leavened bread without consecration is not of any greater excellence than unleavened bread. In commenting on the remark of Leo: *"Azymum vero neque sal neque fermentum habens lutum est aridum,"* the Cardinal sarcastically replied:

> "Si enim, ut definistis, lutum aridum est quidquid neque sal neque fermentum habet; ergo beati spiritus et animae justorum, sive ipsa quatuor elementa, ex quibus omnia visibilia existunt, lutum aridum sunt: quoniam neque sal neque fermentum habent."[40]

In 1054, Dominic, Bishop of Grado and Aquileia, wrote to Peter, Patriarch of Antioch. With wonderful insight and charity he declared that he recognized entirely that the use either of unleavened or of leavened bread is in itself lawful, and he also tried to find parallel reasons to justify this custom.[41]

The IV General Council of the Lateran (1215) assured the Greeks

[37] Hore, *Eighteen Centuries of the Orthodox Greek Church,* p. 395.

[38] Will, *Acta et Scripta,* p. 62.

[39] Will, *op. cit.,* pp. 89-92.

[40] Will, *Acta et Scripta,* p. 105.

[41] *Epistola ad Petrum Antiochensem*: "Nam fermenti et farinae commistio, qua Orientis utuntur ecclesiae, incarnati Verbi declarat substantiam, simplex vero massa azymorum, quam Romana tenet ecclesia, puritatem humanae carnis, quam placuit divinitati sibi unire, citra controversiam repraesentat."—as quoted by Will, *ibid.,* p. 207.

that the Latin Church intended to cherish and honor the maintenance of their customs and rites, as much as, with the help of the Lord, it could do so.[42]

Daniel (1201-1264), Prince of Galicia, and his brother, Basilicus (Vassilko [1203-1269]), Prince of Volhynia, Belz and Vladimir (Wladzimierz), wrote a letter in 1247 to Pope Innocent IV (1243-1254), asking to be restored to union with him. The Pope assured them that there was never any intention of Latinizing the Orientals, and the bishops and priests of their respective countries would be allowed to consecrate in leavened bread according to their use.[43]

St. Thomas Aquinas (1227-1274) stated that it was illicit and sinful for a Latin priest to celebrate Mass in a Latin Church with leavened bread, or for a Greek priest to perform the *Liturgy* in a Greek Church with unleavened bread.[44] At the II General Council of Lyons (1274), Emperor Michael Palaeologus (1259-1282) made a profession of faith in which he declared that the Roman Church uses unleavened bread for bringing the Sacrament of the Eucharist into existence.[45]

Finally, the Reunion Council of Florence (1438-1455) defined it as an article of faith that the Body of Christ is truly consecrated in unleavened or leavened bread made of wheat.[46] Not all the Greeks received this definition: some were happy to heal the break with Rome, and accordingly accepted the decree of the Council wholeheartedly; others accepted it, but after a time lapsed again into schism and repudiated the decree; but the great majority of the Orientals did not even tentatively accept a union with the Pope and the Azymites, as they called Latin Catholics, and were content to remain in schism with their head residing at Constantinople as Patriarch.

[42] Denzinger, *Enchiridion*, n. 435; Mansi, XXII, 989.

[43] Potthast, *Regesta Pontificum Romanorum inde ab anno post Christum natum MCXCVIII (1198) ad annum MCCCIV (1304)* (2 vols., Berolini, 1874-1875), n. 12669, and n. 12688 (hereafter cited *Regesta*); Élie Berger, *Les Registres D'Innocent IV* (4 vols., Parisiis, 1884-1897), I, n. 3223, and n. 3236. Cf. Fortescue, *The Uniate Eastern Churches* (New York: Benziger Brothers, 1923), p. 31; King, *Notes on the Catholic Liturgies*, p. 350.

[44] *Summa Theologica*, III, q. 74, a. 4, *in corpore*.

[45] Denzinger, *Enchiridion*, n. 465; Hardouin, VII, 694s; Mansi, XXIV, 70.

[46] Denzinger, *op. cit.*, n. 692; Mansi, XXXI, B, 1666.

## CHAPTER VI

# THE MIXING OF WATER WITH THE WINE

WITH the exception of the Armenians, all the Rites, Eastern and Western, mix water with the wine before the consecration. The testimony of the first three centuries makes it clear that this practice of mixing water with the wine goes back to the very beginning. There has never been any change in this custom throughout the centuries, and, with the exception of the Armenians and some heretical sects, there has never been any controversy or disagreement on this practice between the Rites.[1] The mixing of water with the wine for the Holy Sacrifice, then, has always been faithfully observed in the Church, with the sole exceptions already indicated.

Pope St. Alexander I (105-115?) is said to have confirmed and sealed the practice of mixing water with the wine, not in that he initially authorized this mingling of the two elements, but inasmuch as in his stand against the errors of heretics he clearly and firmly stated that this practice was received from the Lord and His Apostles.[2]

Some bishops of St. Cyprian's province in North Africa wanted to use wine only in the chalice for the sacrifice of the Mass. Against this abuse St. Cyprian protested vehemently, and insisted on the mixture of wine and water, which Our Lord had used at the Last Supper.[3]

[1] Cardinal Bona thinks that the Armenians used wine to the exclusion of water in their exaggerated opposition to those heretics who used water only—the Ebionites, Encratites, Manicheans and Aquarii or Hydroparasts.—*Res Liturgicae,* lib. II, c. 9, n. 3, p. 368. Cf. Fortescue, *The Mass,* p. 306. It should be noted that the Catholic Armenians use the mixed chalice, that is, wine with a little water added.

[2] *Epistola I—MPG,* V, 1064; Mansi, I, 638; Bona, *op. cit.,* p. 367.

[3] *Epistola LXIII (ad Caecilium)—CSEL,* III, pars 2, 701-717; *MPL,* IV, 374-382. St. Cyprian also stated in this Epistle (c. 13) that the mixing of water with the wine symbolizes the union of the faithful with Christ. The water signifies the faithful, the wine the Blood of Christ.—*CSEL, ibid.,* p. 711. Cf. Apoc., xvii, 15.

The III Council of Carthage (397) legislated that in the Sacrament of the Eucharist nothing else should be offered than what Christ Himself bequeathed, that is, bread and wine *mixed with water*.[4] The second canon of the *Canones Apostolorum* (c. 400) threatened with deposition any priest or bishop who offered upon the altar anything contrary to what Our Lord Himself offered.[5] The Council of Auxerre (578) likewise enacted in its eighth canon that it was not permitted to offer in the Sacrifice of the altar anything except wine mixed with water.[6]

The Council in Trullo (692) condemned the Armenians for not mixing water with the wine used for the Holy Sacrifice. This Council cited the III Council of Carthage (397) that only bread and wine mixed with water were to be offered in the Holy Sacrifice. The Armenians were told to observe the tradition of offering bread and wine mixed with water. They were compared to the Hydroparasts —heretics who offered water only in the Eucharist. The Council in Trullo also threatened with deposition any priest or bishop who did not offer the Holy Sacrifice according to the manner handed down by the Apostles, but who performed an imperfect ministry and introduced innovations.[7]

The Capitulary of Theodolfus, Bishop of Orleans in France, issued to his priests (797), shows that the practice of mixing water with the wine before the consecration was universal. The priests were cautioned to make sure that the bread and wine and water, without which Mass was not to be celebrated, were pure and clean and in no way contaminated.[8] In the Council of Worms (868) there

[4] Canon 32: "Ut in sacramentis corporis et sanguinis Domini nihil amplius offeratur, quam ipse Dominus tradidit, hoc est, panis et vinum aqua mixtum."—Mansi, III, 884; Bona, *op. cit.*, lib. II, c. 9, n. 3, p. 367. Cf. XVI Council of Carthage (419), caput 4—*Fonti*, IX, n. 606; Mansi, IV, 483.

[5] *Fonti*, IX, n. 605; Funk, *Didascalia et Constitutiones Apostolorum* (2 vols., Paderborn, 1905), I, 565.

[6] "Non licet in altario in sacrificio divino mellitum, quod mulsum appellant, nec ullum aliud poculum, extra vinum cum aqua mixtum offerre."—Hardouin, III, 444.

[7] Canon 32—*Fonti*, IX, n. 607; Pitra, *Historia et Monumenta*, II, 39-41; Mansi, XI, 957.

[8] Mansi, XIII, n. 5, 996.

is practically a reiteration of the legislation of the Council of Auxerre. Canon 4 reads as follows:

> Ideoque praeter panem et vinum cum aqua mixtum aliud offerri non debet. Calix enim Dominicus vino et aqua permixtus debet offerri." [9]

Therefore, only bread and wine mixed with water were to be offered in Mass.

In 1202 Pope Innocent III (1198-1216) wrote a letter to John, the Archbishop of Lyons. John had asked the Pope whether the water was converted with the wine into the Blood of Christ at the consecration. The Pope answered that the opinion of the Scholastics differed, but that the more probable opinion was the one which asserted that the water together with the wine is changed into the Precious Blood of Christ.[10]

There were some who went to the other extreme, however, by adding water to the wine in very large quantity. Pope Honorius III (1216-1227) called this practice an exceedingly pernicious abuse. The custom of the universal Church was the reasonable one: it consisted in putting more wine than water into the chalice for the Mass.[11]

The Council of Florence (1438-1445) mentioned in the *Decretum pro Armenis* (1439) that very little water—*aqua modicissima*—ought to be mixed with the wine.[12] The Armenians stubbornly refused to mix any water with their wine. The Trullan Synod of 692 had condemned the Armenians for their refusal to mix some water with their wine when performing the Liturgy, and now the Council of Florence

[9] Hardouin, V, 738.

[10] C. 6, X, *de celebratione Missarum et sacramento Eucharistiae, et divinis officiis*, III, 41; Denzinger, *Enchiridion*, n. 416.

[11] "Perniciosus valde, sicut audivimus, in tuis partibus inolevit abusus, videlicet, quod in maiore quantitate de aqua ponitur in sacrificio quam de vino: cum secundum rationabilem consuetudinem Ecclesiae generalis plus in ipso sit de vino quam de aqua ponendum." C. 13, X, *de celebratione Missarum, et sacramento Eucharistiae, et divinis officiis*, III, 41; Potthast, *Regesta*, n. 6441; Denzinger, *Enchiridion*, n. 441.

[12] This requirement of "very little" water was evidently a concession to Armenian feelings.

strongly upheld the divine and Apostolic tradition, refusing in any way to deviate from it.[13]

The Council of Trent (1545-1563) finally warned the priests to observe the precept of the Church which commanded them to mix water with the wine in the chalice. The Council also appealed to tradition, stating that Christ Himself mixed water with the wine. Furthermore, the Council condemned anyone who maintained that water did not have to be mixed with the wine in the offering of the chalice.[14]

The Orientals have the custom of mixing water *twice* with the wine in the chalice. The first time they mix ordinary water with the wine before beginning the Liturgy, that is, when they prepare the sacred gifts at the *prothesis*.[15] The priest plunges the holy lance into the bread and says: "Unus militum lancea latus eius aperuit, statimque exivit sanguis et equa"; then the deacon pours the wine and water into the chalice. After the consecration, immediately before the Communion, the deacon asks the priest to bless the hot water which is to be poured into the consecrated wine. The priest does so with the words: "Benedictus fervor sanctorum tuorum iugiter, nunc et semper et in saecula saeculorum. Amen." Then the deacon pours the hot water into the chalice saying: "Fervor fidei plenus Spiritu Sancto. Amen."[16]

The addition of the hot water, called *zeon*, into the consecrated chalice appears to have existed among the Byzantines from about the sixth century, for when Heraclius (610-641) had conquered Persia and a great part of Armenia, he invited the schismatic Armenians to a synod of reunion. The Gregorian Catholicos, Moyses, refused the offer saying:

[13] "Tertium est Eucharistiae sacramentum, cuius materia est panis triticeus, et vinum de vite, cui ante consecrationem aqua modicissima admisceri debet."—Denzinger, *op. cit.*, n. 698.

[14] *Sess. XXII, de sanctissimo Missae sacrificio*, c. 7—Denzinger, *op. cit.*, n. 945. And canon 9: "Si quis dixerit, . . . aquam non miscendam esse vino in calice offerendo, eo quod sit contra Christi institutionem: A. S."—Denzinger, *op. cit.*, n. 956.

[15] Equivalent to the credence table of the Latin Church.

[16] Bona, *Res Liturgicae*, lib. II. cap. 9, n. 3, p. 369; O'Brien, *History of the Mass* (New York, 1891), p. 342.

"I decline to cross the river Aza (still in Persia) to be compelled by the Byzantines to eat leavened bread and to drink hot water."[17]

St. Nicephorus, Patriarch of Constantinople (806-815), stated that no priest was permitted to celebrate Mass without hot water except in great necessity, and only if hot water was not available.[18] Furthermore, Innocent IV (1243-1254) in his letter *Sub Catholicae* declared that in pouring the water, whether cold or hot or tepid, in the sacrifice of the altar, the Greeks could follow their custom if they wished, provided that in conformity with the wording of the canon they believed and proclaimed that the Eucharist was derived from the use alike of both the elements of wine and water.[19]

There was a spirited discussion at the Council of Florence about the adding of hot water to the consecrated chalice, for the Latin Fathers severely reprehended it, and were at first fully determined to compel the Greeks to abolish it before the decree for the reunion of the Churches would be made out and ratified. Dorotheus, Bishop of Mitylene, however, made so eloquent and satisfactory a defense of the practice that he gained all the Fathers to his side; and as the Pope himself (Eugene IV [1431-1447]) expressed his admiration for the defense, the custom was approved, and so it was still retained by the Greeks.[20]

[17] King, *Notes on the Catholic Liturgies*, p. 437.

[18] Canon 32: "Quod non licet sacerdoti sine aqua calida missam conficere citra magnam necessitatem, nec nisi calida non reperiatur."—*Fonti*, IX, n. 614; Pitra, *Historia et Monumenta*, II, 330.

[19] "Porro in appositione áquae, sive frigidae, sive calidae, vel tepidae, in altaris sacrificio, suam si velint consuetudinem Graeci sequantur, dummodo credant et asserant quod, servata canonis forma, conficiatur pariter de utraque." —Denzinger, *Enchiridion*, n. 452; Potthast, *Regesta*, n. 15265; Mansi, XXIII, 574.

[20] Cited by O'Brien, *History of the Mass*, p. 342. Cf. *supra*, p. 61. The hot water was added to the Precious Blood to signify the blood and water which flowed from the side of Our Lord after He was pierced with a lance. There was probably a practical reason also in the beginning, namely, that in cold climates the hot water was added to the chalice to melt the Precious Blood in the chalice and keep It in a liquid form until Communion was distributed. Cf. Synod of Mount Lebanon (1736), pars II, cap. xii, n. 7—*Acta et Decreta Sacrorum Conciliorum Recentiorum, Collectio Lacensis* (7 vols., Friburgi Brisgoviae, 1870-1890), II, 190 (hereafter cited *Coll. Lac.*).

# CHAPTER VII

## HOLY COMMUNION

The custom of administering Holy Communion under only one species does not come from the earliest practice of the Church. It has already been said that in the first three centuries the practice of administering Holy Communion under both forms was followed. In connection with the custom of administering Holy Communion in both species, the testimonies of the *Didache,* of St. Justin, of the *Epitaphium Pectorii,* of Origen and of St. Cyprian were cited.[1] The *Epitaphium Pectorii,* Tertullian and Dionysius of Alexandria bear witness, on the other hand, that the Body of Christ was placed into the outstretched hands of the recipient.[2] However, even though the ordinary way of distributing Holy Communion was in both forms, still the reception of Holy Communion in solely one form was recognized as the complete reception of the Lord. Tertullian, Origen and Dionysius of Alexandria give testimony in proof of this, for outside of Mass—in communicating at home and in administering the Viaticum—Holy Communion was administered in the one form alone.[3]

The early practice of distributing Holy Communion in both species continued also in later times as the testimony of many Fathers proves. Some of the Oriental Fathers who spoke of this continued practice are St. Cyril of Jerusalem (d. 386), St. Basil (d. 379), St. John Chrysostom (d. 407), as also does the Trullan Synod in 692, which mentions the specific manner of receiving Holy Communion. Among the Western Fathers who wrote about the distribution of Holy Communion under both forms are St. Ambrose (d. 397), St. Augustine (d. 430), St. Gregory the Great (590-604), and Venerable Bede (d. 735).

St. Ambrose compared the benefits received by the Jews in the desert from the water that flowed from the rock with the effects

[1] Cf. *supra,* pp. 4, 6, 8, 9.

[2] Cf. *supra,* pp. 8, 9, 10.

[3] Cf. *supra,* pp. 9, 10.

produced on Christians by the reception of the Blood of Christ in the Holy Eucharist. The water satisfied the Jews for a short time only, the Blood of Christ satisfies for eternity. The Jews drank and were still thirsty, but when Christians drink the Precious Blood, they cannot thirst again.[4]

St. Augustine bore witness to infant Communion as well as to Communion in both species when he said that infants will be judged according to what they bodily accomplished, that is, at the time when they were in the body, when namely they did or did not receive baptism, when they did or did not eat Christ's flesh, when they did or did not drink His blood.[5] In the work *"De Peccatorum Meritis et Remissione,"* there appears St. Augustine's doctrine that infants like adults must receive Holy Communion, for, as he contends, if the words, "unless you eat the flesh of the Son of Man, and drink his blood you shall not have life in you," did not apply to all alike, infants and adults, then it was in vain that maturer years showed themselves solicitous in the matter.[6]

[4] *De Mysteriis*, lib. I, n. 48: "Illis aqua de petra fluxit, tibi sanguis e Christo: illos ad horam satiavit aqua, te sanguis diluit in aeternum. Iudaeus bibit et sitit, tu cum biberis, sitire, non poteris; et illud in umbra, hoc in veritate."—*MPL*, XVI, 405.

[5] *Epistola CCXVII*, cap. 5, n. 16, 11: "Scimus etiam parvulos secundum ea, quae per corpus gesserunt, recepturos vel bonum vel malum, gesserunt autem non per se ipsos sed per eos, quibus pro illis respondentibus et renuntiare diabolo dicuntur et credere in Deum. Unde et in numero fidelium computantur pertinentes ad sententiam domini dicentes: Qui crediderit et baptizatus fuerit, salvus erit. Propter quod et illis, qui hoc sacramentum non accipiunt, contingit, quod sequitur: Qui autem non crediderit, condemnabitur. Unde et ipsi, sicut dixi, si in illa parva aetate moriuntur, utique secundum ea, quae per corpus gesserunt, id est tempore, quo in corpore fuerunt, quando per corda et ora gestantium crediderunt vel non crediderunt, quando baptizati vel non baptizati sunt, quando carnem Christi manducarunt vel non manducarunt, quando sanguinem biberunt vel non biberunt, secundum haec ergo, quae per corpus gesserunt, non secundum ea, quae, si diu hic viverent, gesturi fuerant iudicantur."—*CSEL*, LVII, 415; *MPL*, XXXIII, 984.

[6] Lib. I, cap. 20, n. 27: "An vero quisquam etiam hoc dicere audebit, quod ad parvulos haec sententia non pertineat, possintque sine participatione corporis hujus et sanguinis in se habere vitam: quia non ait, Qui non manducaverit, sicut de Baptismo, Qui non renatus fuerit, sed ait, Si non manducaveritis, velut eos alloquens qui audire et intelligere poterant, quod utique non valent parvuli?

St. Gregory the Great in the sixth and at the beginning of the seventh century,[7] and Venerable Bede in the eighth century,[8] related that the custom of distributing the Holy Eucharist in both species was practiced in their time.

St. John Chrysostom told of the practice of the people drinking the Blood of the Lord in Communion.[9] And St. Cyril of Jerusalem also spoke of the reception of Holy Communion in both species.[10]

But together with the custom of giving Holy Communion under both species there existed also the practice of distributing Holy Communion under the form of bread alone, even to those who were not sick. Already in the fifth century Pope Leo the Great (440-461) spoke of men who, while secretly holding the doctrines of Manicheism, came to receive the Holy Eucharist, but only in the form of bread.[11]

Evagrius Scholasticus (d. ca. 598) related a custom which was prevalent in Constantinople, namely, that the particles of the Body of Christ which were left over after the Liturgy had been celebrated were given to the children—*pueri impuberes*—to eat.[12]

Sed qui hoc dicit, non attendit quia nisi omnes ista sententia teneat, ut sine corpore et sanguine Filii hominis vitam habere non possint, frustra etiam aetas maior id curat. Potest enim, si non voluntatem, sed verba loquentis attendas, eis solis videri dictum, quibus tunc Dominus loquebatur: quia non ait, Qui non manducaverit; sed, Si non manducaveritis."—*CSEL,* LX, 25-27; *MPL,* XLIV, 124.

[7] *In Septem Psalmos Poenitentiales Expositio Psalmi 109,* n. 11—*MPL,* LXXIX, 640.

[8] *Epistola II, ad Egbertum Antistitem*—*MPL,* XCIV, 665.

[9] *Epistola I, ad Corinthios, Homilia XXVII,* n. 5—*MPG,* LXI, 230.

[10] *Catechesis XXIII, Mystagogica V*: "Tum vero post communionem corporis Christi, accede et ad sanguinis poculum."—*MPG,* XXXIII, 1125.

[11] *Sermo XLII,* c. 5—*MPL,* LIV, 279-280.

[12] *Historia Ecclesiastica,* lib. IV, c. 36—*MPG,* LXXXVI, pars 2, 2769. Duchesne also gives an example of this custom: "Communion at home, a very frequent custom in the time of the persecutions, was maintained among solitaries in monasteries where there were no priests, and, generally, in the case of those who lived at a great distance from a church, even after the Church was free from persecution. In 519, Dorotheos, the Bishop of Thessalonica, fearing that persecution was about to descend upon his flock, caused the elements for communion to be distributed among them in baskets."—Duchesne, *Christian Worship,* p. 249, footnote 3. Duchesne borrows this text from Thiel, *Epistolae*

It must be concluded, then, that neither the administering of Holy Communion under both species nor the administering of It under one species alone was the universal practice in the early Church. Therefore the distribution of Holy Communion in one or in both forms does not belong to the essence of the Sacrament of the Holy Eucharist, nor was it a precept given by Christ to use one form or both in giving Holy Communion to the faithful. It must be said, then, that this matter belonged to the discipline of the Church, and that the Church with its own proper authority could legislate in what way Holy Communion was to be distributed.

Up to the twelfth century Holy Communion was still administered to the faithful under both kinds.[13] After that time the reception under both species gradually became restricted to the celebrant, but the restriction did not become a universal law in the Church until the Council of Constance (1414-1418) in 1415. This Council stated that there were many, namely, the Hussites and Wyclifites, who still rashly asserted that the Christian laity should communicate not only under the species of bread, but also under the species of wine, and that the laity could communicate even after eating a meal or otherwise not fasting, which however was in opposition to the reasonable custom of the Church. The Council then decreed:

> "Hinc est, quod hoc praesens Concilium . . . declarat, decernit et diffinit . . . (sequitur declaratio et praescriptio sacramentum non debere confici post coenam). . . . Et sicut haec consuetudo ad evitandum aliqua pericula et scandala est rationabiliter introducta: quod licet in primitiva Ecclesia huiusmodi sacramentum reciperetur a fidelibus sub utraque specie, tamen postea a conficientibus sub utraque et a laicis tantummodo sub specie panis suscipiatur, cum firmissime credendum sit et nullatenus dubitandum, integrum Christi corpus et sanguinem tam sub specie panis, quam sub specie vini veraciter contineri. . . ."[14]

The error of Martin Luther (1483-1546) which stated that the Church should take conciliar action in order to have the laity re-

*Romanorum Pontificum a Sancto Hilario (461-468) usque ad Sanctum Hormisdam (514-523)* (Brunsbergae, 1868), p. 902, n. 2.

[13] Romsée, *Praxis Celebrandi Missam* (5 vols. in 4, Leodii, 1791), IV, 402.

[14] Denzinger, *Enchiridion*, n. 626; Hardouin, VIII, 381 B; Mansi, XXVII, 727 C.

ceive Holy Communion under both species was condemned by Pope Leo X (1513-1521) in his Bull, *Exsurge Domine,* issued in 1520.[15]

Finally, the Council of Trent in Session XXI, *de Communione sub utraque specie, et parvulorum,* chapter 1, approved and defined that the laity and the non-celebrating clergy were not obliged by any divine precept to receive the Holy Eucharist under both species, and that Holy Communion under one species was sufficient for salvation. In chapter 2 of the same session the Council recognized and declared that, although it was the common custom from the beginning of Christianity to receive Holy Communion in both species, nevertheless, through the progress of time, that custom was changed in view of grave and just causes. The Council therefore approved the custom of communicating under one kind, and decreed this as law, which could not allowably be reprobated or changed at will without the authority of the Church.[16]

The Council also, in issuing three dogmatic canons concerning Holy Communion under both species, condemned anyone who maintained that the faithful could receive the Holy Eucharist only under both species, but not under the form of bread alone, for the reason that Christ was present whole and entire only under both species.[17]

This was the law enacted for the Western Church. Thus while the custom of receiving the Holy Eucharist under both forms disappeared in the West, and the practice was finally even condemned, the East retained the practice of giving Holy Communion in the double form of bread and of wine.

[15] Denzinger, *op. cit.,* n. 756.

[16] Denzinger, *Enchiridion,* nn. 930, 931.

[17] Canon 1: "Si quis dixerit, ex Dei praecepto vel ex necessitate salutis omnes et singulos Christi fideles utramque speciem sanctissimi Eucharistiae sacramenti sumere debere: anathema sit."—Denzinger, *op. cit.,* n. 934.

Canon 2: "Si quis dixerit, sanctam Ecclesiam catholicam non iustis causis et rationibus adductam fuisse, ut laicos, atque etiam clericos non conficientes, sub una panis tantummodo specie communicaret, aut in eo errasse: A. S."—Denzinger, *op. cit.,* n. 935.

Canon 3: "Si quis negaverit, totum et integrum Christum, omnium gratiarum fontem et auctorem, sub una panis specie sumi, quia, ut quidam falso asserunt, non secundum ipsius Christi institutionem sub utraque specie sumatur: A. S."—Denzinger, *op. cit.,* n. 936.

There were three ways of giving Holy Communion in both species: the first way was to give the sacred Host to the communicant, who received it in his hands, and then to offer the chalice from which the communicant drank. This was the practice followed in the early Church, as the testimony of the Fathers indicates.[18] At a later time women had to cover their hand with a white cloth, although the men still received the Holy Eucharist in their bare hand.[19] The manner in which the communicant was to receive the Holy Eucharist was prescribed by the Council in Trullo (692): "Manus in crucis formam figurans, sic accedat, et gratiae communionem accipiat."[20] The hands were to be held out to receive the Holy Body of Christ with the left hand held under the right hand as a kind of support. The Council stated further that it was not permitted to use a receptacle, even of gold or of any other metal, to receive the divine gift, instead of receiving the sacred Host in the hands. Venerable Bede (d. 735) likewise spoke of the reception of Holy Communion in the hand.[21]

The second way of distributing Holy Communion was for the priest to place the sacred Host in the hand of each communicant, while the deacon followed with the Chalice to administer the Precious Blood with the aid of a small spoon which he dipped into the chalice and then placed in the mouth of the recipient.[22] The deacon played an important part in the Eucharistic Sacrifice in the beginning. But at times the deacons went too far by assuming an importance beyond their rank, so that they had to be made to realize their position in the hierarchy. The I General Council of Nicaea (325) condemned the deacons for receiving Holy Communion before the bishops and

[18] E. g., *Epitaphium Pectorii*, Tertullian, St. Cyprian, and Dionysius of Alexandria.

[19] St. Augustine, *Sermo CCXXIX*, 5—*MPL*, XXXIX, 2168. The Council of Auxerre (578), in canon 42, calls this cloth the *dominicale.*—Hefele-Leclercq, *Histoire des Conciles* (10 tomes in 19 vols., Paris, 1907-1938), II, 220.

[20] Canon 101—*Fonti*, IX, n. 265; Pitra, *Historia et Monumenta*, II, 70-71; Mansi, XI, 985.

[21] *Historia Ecclesiastica*, IV, 24—*MPL*, XCV, 214.

[22] Tertullian, *De Corona*, c. 3—*MPL*, II, 80, and St. Cyprian, *De Lapsis*, c. 22—*MPL*, IV, 483.

priests, and for administering Communion to them.[23] The custom of allowing the deacon to distribute Holy Communion disappeared in both the East and the West, although he still received the authority to do so when he was ordained a deacon. The use of the spoon in distributing the Precious Blood gave way to a tube of gold or silver as a caution against the possible spilling of the sacred species.[24] Each one of the faithful had his own tube.[25]

In consequence of abuses which had arisen, the offering of the chalice to the people was forbidden, and a third method of distributing Holy Communion came into use. The consecrated bread was dipped into the Precious Blood and then administered to the communicant with a spoon. In this case there was no separate receiving of the Precious Blood. This method was called *Intinction.* It became the common practice for the distribution of Holy Communion. It still remains in the East, though Pope Paschal II (1099-1118) had objected to this custom as a humanly derived innovation which might give occasion for the people to think that the content of the chalice became consecrated through its contact with the Body of Our Lord.[26]

The spread, from the twelfth to the fourteenth century in the West, of the custom of receiving Holy Communion in one kind, which was later made law by the Council of Constance and thereupon confirmed by the Council of Trent, removed the danger of the spilling of the Precious Blood, neutralized the otherwise present fear of impending irreverence to the Holy Eucharist, and effectively promoted the proper consideration for cleanliness and hygiene in the administration of the Eucharist to the people. The new practice and law likewise lessened the mental worries of those who in duty had to be most concerned about the proper custody and due reverence of the Holy Eucharist.

[23] Canon 18—Mansi, II, 675.

[24] This tube was called a *fistula.* Cf. Bona, *Res Liturgicae,* I, 238.

[25] The people partook of the Precious Blood from a chalice different from the one used by the celebrant until that practice was forbidden by Pope Gregory II (715-731). The chalice used by the priest was called the Offertorial Chalice; the one used for the people was called the Ministerial Chalice.—Meagher, *The Seven Gates of Heaven,* p. 198.

[26] *Epistola DXXXV—MPL,* CLXIII, 442; Mansi, XX, 1013.

For a long time it was customary to communicate children under the species of wine immediately after their baptism. This the priest accomplished by dipping his finger into the Precious Blood and then letting the child suck it. That the new-born children received Holy Communion was attested by St. Cyprian (d. 258), St. Augustine (d. 430) and the Church historian Evagrius (d. ca. 598).[27] Like testimony was given by Gennadius (d. 485) [28] and Pseudo-Dionysius (c. 500), who related that infants received the Holy Eucharist immediately after they were baptized.[29]

The II Council of Mâcon, in 585, ordered that all the consecrated hosts that remained should be given to the children on Wednesday or Friday. The children were to be fasting, but the priests could dip the hosts in wine to enable the children to swallow them more easily.[30]

In the Western Church, when the custom of administering baptism to a large group of infants on Holy Saturday ceased in about the twelfth century, the administration of Holy Communion to infants also ceased. This practice of the non-administration of Holy Communion to infants was confirmed in the next century by the IV General Council of the Lateran (1215), which prescribed who should receive Holy Communion and when. In canon 21 the Council ordered:

> "Omnis utriusque sexus fidelis, postquam ad annos discretionis pervenerit, omnia sua solus peccata saltem semel in anno fideliter confiteatur proprio sacerdoti, et iniunctam sibi poenitentiam pro viribus studeat adimplere, suscipiens reverenter ad minus in Pascha Eucharistiae sacramentum . . ." [31]

[27] St. Cyprian, *De Lapsis*, n. 25—*MPL*, IV, 484s; St. Augustine, *De Peccatorum Meritis et Remissione*, lib. I, cap. 20, n. 27—*CSEL*, LX, 25-27, *MPL*, XLIV, 124; Evagrius, *Historiae Ecclesiasticae*—*MPG*, LXXXVI, pars II, 2770.

[28] *De Ecclesiasticis Dogmatibus*, c. 52—*MPL*, LVIII, 993.

[29] *De Ecclesiastica Hierarchia*, c. 7, n. 11: "Quod autem infantes quoque qui per aetatem nequeunt intelligere, divinae regenerationis, sanctissimorumque divinae communionis mysteriorum participes fiant."—*MPG*, III, 566.

[30] Canon 6: "Quaecumque reliquiae sacrificiorum post peractam Missam in sacrario supersederint, quarta vel sexta feria innocentes ab illo cujus interest, ad ecclesiam adducantur, et indicto eis jejunio, easdem reliquias conspersas vino percipiant."—Mansi, IX, 952.

[31] Denzinger, *Enchiridion*, n. 437.

The Council of Trent in Session XXI, *de Communione sub utraque specie, et parvulorum,* chapter 4, legislated that it was not necessary for infants who lacked the use of reason—*parvuli*—to receive Sacramental Communion, but likewise that those who practiced this custom in the early days of the Church were not to be condemned. The Council however did condemn those who maintained that this practice had still to be observed:

> "Si quis dixerit, parvulis, antequam ad annos discretionis pervenerint, necessariam esse Eucharistiae communionem: anathema sit." [32]

In the Eastern Church the practice of administering Holy Communion to infants remained. If possible, the baptism took place during the Liturgy, so that the newly baptized child might be brought to the altar to receive Holy Communion in the form of wine. The same was sometimes done when a child was in danger of death, Holy Communion being administered as Viaticum, lest the child die without the benefit of the Holy Eucharist.

[32] Sess. XXI, *De Communione sub utraque specie, et parvulorum,* can. 4—Denzinger, *Enchiridion,* n. 937.

# CHAPTER VIII

## SUMMARY

From the time of the I Council of Nicaea (325) until the Council of Trent (1545-1563) the greater modification of discipline in relation to the Holy Eucharist took place in the Western Church. The Eastern Church, for the most part, held to the traditions of the early Church. But there were changes in both Churches. Laws were passed regarding the matter to be used in the celebration of Mass, the altar on which the Holy Sacrifice was to be offered and the manner to be employed in the distributing of Holy Communion, and many of these laws still bind today.

During the twelve centuries of this period it was definitely settled that the bread could be leavened or unleavened according to the Rite of the priest celebrating the Eucharistic Sacrifice. The Eastern Church also continued to add hot water to the Precious Blood before the Communion. An Oriental priest had to celebrate the Liturgy on an *Antimension,* whether the altar was consecrated or not. A Latin priest had to celebrate Mass on a consecrated altar or altar-stone. Holy Communion was to be distributed only in the form of bread in the Western Church, while in the Eastern Church the Holy Eucharist continued to be administered in both species. The practice of not administering Holy Communion to infants was confirmed by the IV General Council of the Lateran (1215) and this Council of the Lateran and the Council of Trent (1545-1563) legislated that only those who had attained the use of reason were obliged to receive the Holy Eucharist. The Council of Trent also condemned anyone who said that children who had not as yet attained the use of reason were nevertheless obliged to receive Holy Communion.

# PART III

## From the Council of Trent (1545-1563) to the Present Time (1946)

### CHAPTER I

### THE MATTER OF THE HOLY EUCHARIST

#### Article I. The Eucharistic Bread: Unleavened and Leavened

The Council of Florence (1438-1445) had settled the dispute between the Eastern and the Western Church about the validity of unleavened bread as matter for the Holy Eucharist. That Council had condemned the error of the Eastern Schismatics who declared that unleavened bread was invalid matter, and had defined it as an article of faith that the Body of Christ was truly consecrated either in leavened or unleavened bread. Furthermore, priests were to consecrate the Body of the Lord in either, each according to the use of his Church, whether Eastern or Western.[1]

Since the Council of Florence there exist many Papal documents instructing the Orientals to follow their own Rite and to preserve studiously and carefully the habits, institutions, rites and customs which they had received from their Greek fathers, and to show to the Roman Church only due obedience and reverence.[2]

With regard to the matter for the Holy Eucharist, the Popes for

[1] Eugenius IV, *Decretum pro Graecis,* § 4—*Codicis Iuris Canonici Fontes cura Emi Petri Card. Gasparri editi* (9 vols., Romae, [postea Civitate Vaticana]: Typis Polyglottis Vaticanis, 1923-1939), (Vols. VII, VIII, et IX ed. cura et studio Emi Iustiniani Card. Serédi), n. 51 (hereafter cited *Fontes*). Cf. Denzinger, *Enchiridion,* n. 692.

[2] Cf. Benedictus XIV, const. *Etsi pastoralis,* 26 maii, 1742, Proemium—*Fontes,* n. 328; *Collectanea Sacrae Congregationis de Propaganda Fide* (2 vols., Romae, 1907), n. 338 (hereafter cited *Collect.*).

the most part simply reiterated the law of the Council of Florence. Pope Gregory XIII (1572-1585), in the profession of faith drawn up for the Greeks, used the very words of the Council when prescribing belief in the validity of unleavened bread for consecration:

> "Item in azymo, sive fermentato pane triticeo corpus Christi veraciter confici. Sacerdotesque in altero ipsum Domini corpus conficere debere, unumquemque scilicet iuxta suae Ecclesiae, sive Occidentalis, sive Orientalis consuetudinem."[3]

The same is true of the profession of faith which Pope Benedict XIV (1740-1758) drew up for the Maronites and sent to the Maronite Archbishop, Simon of Damascus. The profession expresses belief in the Councils of the Church and in their teaching. One of the articles of the profession is the teaching of the Council of Florence about the validity of unleavened bread for consecration.[4]

After the fall of Constantinople (1453), many Greeks had fled to Italy and to the surrounding islands. They were received with hospitality and were never asked by the Popes to change the rites which they used. They were rather instructed to observe faithfully their own Rite, and were warned not to modify or latinize any of the ancient principles of their Rite. The Constitution *Etsi pastoralis* of Pope Benedict XIV was addressed to these Greeks in particular, but the instructions and warning were extended to all Orientals. The Pope likewise cited the law of the Council of Florence regarding the validity of unleavened and leavened bread for the Holy Sacrifice, although he did not quote the Council verbatim.[5]

Since the Council of Florence had legislated that priests were to consecrate the Body of the Lord according to the use of their own Church, either in leavened or unleavened bread, Pope Benedict XIV gravely forbade a Latin priest to use the Greek Rite, and a Greek priest to use the Latin Rite, in offering the Holy Sacrifice.

[3] Const. *Sanctissimus*, a. 1575, Professio fidei Graecis praescr., § 3—*Fontes*, n. 146.

[4] Ep. *Nuper ad Nos*, 16 mart. 1743, Professio fidei Maronitis praescr., § 5—*Fontes*, n. 335.

[5] Const. *Etsi pastoralis*, 26 maii, 1742, § I, n. II—*Fontes*, n. 328; *Collect.*, n. 338.

This was forbidden under penalty of perpetual suspension *"a divinis."* [6]

In the encyclical letter *Allatae sunt* there is contained some of the most important legislation of Pope Benedict XIV for the Orientals. This encyclical was addressed to missionaries in the Near East, chiefly in Syria and Asia Minor. The missionaries were to convert Eastern schismatics to the Catholic faith; to fight against errors; but in no way were they to try to make their converts Latins. The laws did not allow the mixing of Rites. Priests of the Eastern Rites when there were no churches of their own Rite in a place could, of course, celebrate the Liturgy in Latin Churches, but in that case too they had to follow their own Rite exactly.[7]

In speaking about the bread to be used for the Holy Eucharist, the Pope said that Greeks and Orientals, if they wished to be counted as Catholics, had to profess that both unleavened bread as well as leavened bread was valid matter for the Sacrament of the Eucharist, and everyone had to adhere to the Rite of his Church. Whoever rejected as heretical the Rite of the Latin Church, which used unleavened bread for the consecration of the Holy Eucharist, departed from the truth and lapsed into error.[8]

There were some Greeks and Orientals who, for the most part, retained their own Rite, but nevertheless not only revered the Latin Rite and the other Western Rites but even followed some of their customs. These Orientals also followed ancient customs which were fully known and approved by their Bishops, and also expressly or tacitly confirmed by the Holy See. Among them were the Armenians and the Maronites, who did not use leavened bread but unleavened.[9]

The use of unleavened bread by the Maronites and Armenians was a very old and immemorial custom, as the National Synod of the Maronites on Mount Lebanon, in 1736, stated: "This custom was observed from time immemorial, both in our Church and also

[6] *Ibid.*, § VI, n. X—*Fontes*, n. 328; *Collect.*, n. 338.

[7] Ep. encycl. *Allatae sunt*, 26 iul. 1755, §§ 4, 33, 35, 36— *Fontes*, n. 434; *Collect.*, n. 395.

[8] *Ibid.*, § 22—*Fontes*, n. 434; *Collect.*, n. 395.

[9] *Ibid.*, § 23—*Fontes*, n. 434; *Collect.*, n. 395.

among the Armenians in the East, and we can produce authentic documents of this." [10]

The Synod of Zamość, which was held in 1720, legislated according to the Council of Florence that the matter for the Sacrament of the Eucharist in the Oriental Church is only leavened bread made from wheat, and wine made from grapes. Moreover, the Synod added a sanction: any priest who used any other bread or wine in celebrating the Divine Liturgy was to be suspended *"a divinis,"* removed from office and punished by the bishop.[11]

In 1902 the Sacred Congregation for the Propagation of the Faith demanded that the Nestorian bishops and priests who wished to become Catholics first had to be instructed in the points of faith about which they were ignorant or which they knew only in a confused manner. Monsignor Henry Altmayer, Apostolic Delegate in Mesopotamia, drew up a profession of faith containing the dogmas which the converts had to believe and confess. Among the dogmas was one which referred to the matter of the Holy Eucharist. This article stated that the valid matter required for the valid consecration of the Body of Our Lord in the Eucharist was wheaten bread, whether leavened or unleavened.[12]

The law of the Council of Florence was again quoted and stressed by Pope Pius X in the Constitution *Tradita ab antiquis.* In this Constitution the Pope made provisions for Catholics who were in a

[10] Synod of Mount Lebanon (1736), pars II, cap. xii, n. 7: "Qui mos, in Ecclesia nostra, et apud Armenos quoque in Oriente, ab immemorabili tempore obtinuit, et authentica etiam hujus rei documenta proferre possumus."—*Coll. Lac.*, II, 190. Besides the Armenians and Maronites, the Chaldeans in Malabar, the Syro-Malabars and the Italo-Greeks in a few churches in Sicily, in southern Italy, and in places belonging to the monastery of the Mother of God at Grottaferrata also used unleavened bread. Cf. Ep. Encycl. *Allatae sunt,* § 23, and S. C. de Prop. Fide, decr. 20 nov. 1838—*Fontes,* n. 4777; *Collect.*, n. 878.

[11] Synod of Zamość (1720), tit. III, § 3, a—*Fonti,* XI, *Ius Particulare Ruthenorum,* 253. The enactments of the Synod of Zamość were confirmed by Pope Benedict XIII on July 19, 1724, and bound only certain Ruthenian dioceses.—Const. *Apostolatus officium—Fonti,* XI, 765; *Coll. Lac.*, II, 2-3. But on February 22, 1807, Pope Pius VII confirmed the enactments of the Synod and extended them to the entire Ruthenian Church.—Const. *In universalis Ecclesiae regimine,* n. 11—*Fonti,* XI, 766.

[12] Instr. 31 iul. 1902, n. I, 2—*Fontes,* n. 4940; *Collect.*, n. 2149.

place where there was no church of their own Rite. He wanted them to know that the Body of Our Lord, whether consecrated by a Greek priest in leavened bread or by a Latin priest in unleavened bread, was truly present on the altar, and they were not to hesitate in the act of adoring Him.[13]

The question whether a priest of the Latin Rite could licitly use leavened bread when he celebrated Mass in a church of an Oriental Rite, or whether a priest of an Oriental Rite could licitly use unleavened bread when he performed the Liturgy in a Latin Church, was disputed by theologians. The Church demanded that a priest obtain permission to use a church of another Rite,[14] and that he celebrate Mass in his own Rite.[15] Some theologians thought that a priest was bound to use the Rite of the church in which he celebrated Mass, and that a priest of the Latin Rite had to use fermented bread when he celebrated Mass in an Oriental Church, while an Oriental priest was bound to use unleavened bread when he celebrated in a Latin Church.[16] Other theologians were of the opinion, which Saint Alphonsus (1696-1787) called the common and most probable one, that when a priest celebrated Mass in a church of a different Rite, he could use either unleavened bread or leavened bread, whichever he wished to use.[17]

However, the most acceptable opinion was the one expressed by

[13] Const. *Tradita ab antiquis,* 14 sept. 1912—*Fontes,* n. 698.

[14] A Latin priest had to obtain permission from the pastor of the Oriental Church, and an Oriental priest had to have permission from the Latin Ordinary. —Benedictus XIV, const. *Etsi pastoralis,* § VI, n. VIII; § XI, n. XVI—*Fontes,* n. 328.

[15] Const. *Etsi pastoralis,* § VI, n. X—*Fontes,* n. 328; *Collect.,* n. 338; ep. encycl. *Allatae sunt,* 26 iul. 1755, §§ 4, 33, 35, 36—*Fontes,* n. 434; *Collect.,* n. 395.

[16] Petrus Ledesma, *De Eucharistia,* lib. IV, p. 1, q. 15, art. 4, d. 1, apud Collegium Salmanticensium, *Cursus Theologia Moralis* (6 toms. in 3, Venetiis, 1728), tom. I, tract. iv, cap. 4, punctum 1, n. 20. Ledesma is also cited by Gasparri (*De Eucharistia,* II, n. 805).

[17] Alphonsus de Liguori, *Theologia Moralis* (2 vols., Romae: Augustae Taurinorum ex typis H. Marietti, 1891), lib. VI, n. 203; Franciscus Suarez, *Opera Omnia* (28 vols., Parisiis, 1856-1878. Vol. XX, 1866), Vol. XX, quaest. LXXIV, art. 4, disp. xliv, sect. 3, n. 13; Ledesma, *loc. cit.*

a third group of theologians, who stated that a priest of the Latin Rite who celebrated Mass in a church of an Oriental Rite, not only could, but also had to offer the Eucharistic Sacrifice in unleavened bread; and a priest of an Oriental Rite who performed the Liturgy in a church of the Latin Rite, not only could, but had to use leavened bread.[18] This opinion is in conformity with the prescriptions of the various synods and with the constitutions of the Popes which insisted that priests were to consecrate the Body of the Lord either in unleavened bread or in leavened bread, each according to the use of his church, whether Eastern or Western.[19]

The Code finally settled this dispute among the theologians. In canon 816 it approved the opinion which stated that a priest was to use the bread proper to his own Rite *wherever* he celebrated Mass.

> "In Missae celebratione, sacerdos secundum proprium ritum, debet panem azymum vel fermentatum adhibere ubicunque Sacrum litet."

The words of this canon, *"ubicunque Sacrum litet,"* indicate that a priest of the Latin Rite, or a priest of an Oriental Rite which uses unleavened bread, must always use unleavened bread whenever he celebrates Mass in a church of an Oriental Rite, even if that church is in Oriental territory. The same is true when an Oriental priest who belongs to a Rite which uses leavened bread celebrates the Liturgy in a church of the Latin Rite, or in a church of an Oriental Rite which uses unleavened bread; he must always use leavened bread no matter where that church is located.

It could happen that a priest might be without the bread of his own Rite and thus be unable to celebrate Mass on Sunday for the faithful. Could the priest in this case use the bread of another

[18] Gasparri, *De Eucharistia,* II, n. 805; Gabriel Vasquez, *Commentaria ac Disputationes in Tertiam Partem Sancti Thomae* (3 vols., Lugduni, 1631), tom. III, quaest. lxxiv, art. 4, disp. clxxiv, c. 3.

[19] Eugenius IV, *Decretum pro Graecis,* § 4—*Fontes,* n. 51; Denzinger, *Enchiridion,* n. 692. Cf. Gregorius XIII, const. *Sanctissimus,* a. 1575, Professio fidei Graecis praescr., § 3—*Fontes,* n. 146. Const. *Etsi pastoralis,* § I, n. II—*Fontes,* n. 328; ep. encycl. *Allatae sunt,* 26 iul. 1755, §§ 33, 35, et praesertim, § 36—*Fontes,* n. 434; Synod of Zamość, tit. III, § 3, a—*Fonti,* XI, 253.

Rite in order that the people might fulfill the precept of hearing Mass on Sunday? [20]

In this supposition one is confronted with two conflicting ecclesiastical laws, the one commanding the faithful to hear Mass on Sunday, and the other commanding a priest to use the bread proper to his own Rite wherever he celebrates Mass. The faithful do not violate the Sunday precept if it is impossible for them to fulfill that precept. If the priest may not use bread which is matter proper to another Rite to celebrate Mass on Sunday, then it will be impossible for the faithful to hear Mass, and they are thereby exempted from fulfilling their obligation.

The Code nowhere contains any legislation which permits a priest to consecrate bread that is proper to another Rite, even in the case of necessity. However, according to canon 1245, § 1, the ordinary or the pastor can dispense, for a just cause, in individual cases, individual persons or individual families subject to him, or visitors in his territory, from the law of canon 1248 obliging them to hear Mass on Sundays and holydays of obligation.[21] The law of canon 816 commanding a priest to consecrate bread that is proper to his own Rite, wherever he celebrates Mass, then, takes precedence over the law of canon 1248 commanding the people to hear Mass on Sundays and holydays of obligation.

The obligation of canon 816 is a grave one and binds Oriental priests as well as Latin priests under pain of mortal sin. Although a priest would validly consecrate with leavened or unleavened bread, nevertheless a Latin priest, or an Oriental priest who belongs to a Rite which uses unleavened bread,[22] is bound under pain of mortal

[20] Cf. canon 1248.

[21] Even though such a dispensation were given to the whole congregation, because the reason for the dispensation was valid for all, the dispensation could be considered as being given to each one individually. Cf. Udalricus Beste (*Introductio in Codicem* [2. ed., Collegeville, Minn.: St. John's Abbey Press, 1944], p. 606): "Nihil tamen obstat, quin ob causam sufficientem pluribus communem dispensatio his omnibus unico actu tribuatur. Talis dispensatio, licet virtualiter multiplex, potest adhuc censeri singulis distributiva data ideoque vere dici concessa in casibus singularibus." Cf. also Ayrinhac, *Administrative Legislation*, p. 93.

[22] The Armenians, Maronites, Chaldeans in Malabar, Syro-Malabars, Italo-

sin to consecrate in unleavened bread. An Oriental priest who belongs to one of the other Rites, which consecrates in leavened bread is bound by the same obligation to use leavened bread wherever he celebrates the Liturgy.[23]

In a case of necessity, could a Latin priest (who must use unleavened bread), or a priest of an Oriental Rite which must use unleavened bread, consecrate in leavened bread? And in similar necessity, could an Oriental priest who must use leavened bread consecrate in unleavened bread? When the case of necessity is the completion of the Divine Sacrifice, authors unanimously agree that the priest may use bread that is proper to another Rite.[24] If a priest has already consecrated the chalice and then discovers that the bread which he used is corrupt or invalid matter for Mass, and there is no other bread available but that which is proper to another Rite, then the priest can licitly consecrate bread of another Rite in order to complete the sacrifice.[25]

Greeks in a few churches in Sicily, in southern Italy and in places belonging to the monastery of the Mother of God at Grottaferrata.—Ep. encycl. *Allatae sunt*, § 23—*Fontes*, n. 434.

[23] Cf. The Synod of Zamość, *supra*, p. 61.

[24] Felix M. Cappello, *Tractatus Canonico-Moralis de Sacramentis* (3 vols. in 6, Romae: Marietti, 1932-1945), Vol. I (4. ed., 1945), n. 261 (hereafter cited Cappello, *De Sacramentis*); Gasparri, *De Eucharistia*, II, n. 804; Dominicus Prümmer, *Manuale Theologiae Moralis* (7. ed., 3 vols., Friburgi Brisgoviae: Herder & Co., 1931), III, n. 171 (hereafter cited *Theologia Moralis*); Augustinus Lehmkuhl, *Theologia Moralis* (11. ed., 2 vols., Friburgi Brisgoviae: Herder & Co., 1910), II, n. 165, § 4; Henry Davis, *Moral and Pastoral Theology* (4. ed., 4 vols., New York: Sheed & Ward, 1943), III, 121, sect. 3; Benedictus Henricus Merkelbach, *Summa Theologiae Moralis* (2. ed., 3 vols., Parisiis: Desclée, DeBrouwer et Soc., 1936), III, n. 219; H. Noldin—A. Schmitt, *Summa Theologiae Moralis iuxta Codicem Iuris Canonici* (26. ed., 3 vols., Oeniponte/Lipsiae: Felician Rauch, 1940), III, n. 107, § 1 (hereafter cited *Theologia Moralis*); Eduardus Genicot—I. Salsmans, *Institutiones Theologiae Moralis* (12. ed., 2 vols., Bruxellis: L'Edition Universele, S. A., 1936), II, n. 170 (hereafter cited *Theologia Moralis*).

[25] The phrase, "*to complete the sacrifice*," ordinarily is not understood in this sense. "*To complete the sacrifice*" usually means that the bread has already been consecrated, but for some reason the celebrant is unable to continue on to the consecration of the wine and another priest is obliged to take his place, to consecrate the wine and to finish the Mass.

Can a priest consecrate bread that is proper to another Rite when the case of necessity is that of administering Holy Viaticum to the dying? Many moral theologians agree with Saint Alphonsus who was of the opinion that a priest acts illicitly when he consecrates bread which is proper to another Rite, even if this be necessary for administering Holy Viaticum.[26] The reasons which they give for this opinion are: first, that the reverence due to so great a sacrament should be preferred to the consideration of one's neighbor, to whom this sacrament is not absolutely necessary; [27] and secondly, that the common good, on account of which the Church has strictly decreed that everyone must observe his own Rite, prevails over the private good of the individual.

However, the opposite opinion, namely, that a priest can consecrate bread that is proper to another Rite in order to administer Holy Viaticum to the dying, seems to be equally as probable and a safe norm to follow. Authors generally agree that the obligation to receive Holy Viaticum in danger of death is a precept of the divine law.[28] Therefore, the authors who hold the opinion that a priest may consecrate bread that is proper to another Rite in order to administer Holy Viaticum argue that it is reasonable to suppose that an ecclesiastical law does not bind when there is conflict with a divine precept. A divine precept urges the reception of Holy Viaticum, and thus prevails over the ecclesiastical law stated in

[26] Alphonsus de Liguori, *Theologia Moralis*, lib. VI, n. 203; Genicot, *loc. cit.*; Merkelbach, *loc. cit.*; Noldin, *loc. cit.*

[27] Alphonsus de Liguori: "Ratio, quia in hoc casu praeferenda est reverentia erga tantum sacramentum utilitati proximi, cui tale sacramentum non est simpliciter necessarium." In giving this reason, St. Alphonsus seems to have in mind the precepts to love God and to love one's neighbor. He thought, then, that the reverence due to God present in the Sacrament of the Holy Eucharist demanded that a priest should not illicitly consecrate bread of another Rite even for administering Holy Viaticum to one who is dying, since the reception of Holy Communion is not absolutely necessary for salvation.

[28] Cappello, *ibid.*, n. 421, § 2; Davis, *ibid.*, 227; Prümmer, *ibid.*, n. 208, § 2; Merkelbach, *ibid.*, n. 294, b; Noldin, *ibid.*, n. 137, § 1; Lehmkuhl, *ibid.*, n. 195; A. Tanquerey, *Synopsis Theologiae Dogmaticae* (3 vols., Parisiis: Desclée et Socii, Vol. III, 21. ed., 1929), III, n. 918.

canon 816, which commands a priest to use leavened or unleavened bread, according to his own Rite, *wherever* he celebrates Mass.[29]

Cappello thinks that it is lawful for a priest to celebrate Mass with bread of another Rite because of the milder discipline of the Church as now expressed in canons 851 and 866. Canon 851 permits a priest to administer the Holy Eucharist consecrated in another Rite in the case of necessity, when no priest of that Rite is available. Canon 866 allows the faithful to receive Holy Communion which was consecrated in another Rite, even to satisfy their devotion, and to receive Holy Viaticum consecrated in another Rite, in a case of necessity.[30]

Besides the reasons given that a divine precept prevails over an ecclesiastical law, and that because of the milder discipline of the Church it is lawful for a priest to consecrate bread that is proper to another Rite in order that he may administer Holy Viaticum in the case of necessity, Cappello presents another argument. He argues from the silence of the Code that a priest can consecrate bread which is proper to another Rite in order to administer Holy Viaticum. The Code contains no explicit or implicit prohibition concerning the consecration of the bread of another Rite in order to administer Holy Viaticum. According to a rule of law cited by Cappello, "*Legislator, quod voluit, expressit; quod noluit, tacuit,*" the Code could have made some mention of this prohibition in canon 817. This canon gravely forbids a priest to consecrate one species without the other, or to consecrate both species outside of Mass, and this is forbidden even in the case of extreme necessity. The canon makes no explicit or implicit mention of using only unleavened bread in the case of extreme necessity, or of not using leavened bread in the same case, which the canon could have done.[31]

The only times, then, that a priest may consecrate bread that is proper to another Rite are: when it is necessary for him to com-

[29] Cappello, *ibid.*, n. 261; Prümmer, *ibid.*, n. 171, a; Davis, *ibid.*, 121; Woywod (*A Practical Commentary on the Code of Canon Law* [7. ed., 2 vols., New York: Joseph F. Wagner, 1943], I, n. 718) also seems to lean toward this opinion.

[30] *Loc. cit.*

[31] *Loc. cit.*

plete the Divine Sacrifice; [32] and when it is necessary for him to administer Holy Viaticum. However, a priest can also consecrate bread which is matter proper to another Rite if he has an apostolic indult. Gasparri stated that in practice an apostolic indult was necessary in order that a priest might consecrate bread which is proper to another Rite. But this indult, he continued, was never granted "*per modum actus*" but was sometimes given for a certain time, even without the requirement of a transfer to another Rite.[33]

### Article II. The Mixing of Water with the Wine.

In the decree for the Armenians the Council of Florence legislated that a few drops of water—*aqua modicissima*—were to be mixed with the wine before the consecration.[34] At a later time the Sacred Congregation for the Propagation of the Faith recounted the reasons for the addition of the water to the wine: it was a custom which derived from Apostolic times, for Christ Himself had added water to the wine; it symbolized the two natures in Christ, and therefore those who omitted the practice of adding some water to the wine frequently were involved in the Monophysite heresy, or at least laid themselves open to the suspicion of that heresy; the Council of Florence had decreed that a little water was to be mixed with the wine; and the Holy See always refused to grant permission to anyone who asked whether he could forego following that practice.[35]

The Holy Office was asked whether a schismatic Armenian priest who became a Catholic could in any way be dispensed from *publicly* adding water to the chalice in the celebration of Mass, provided that he did so secretly in the sacristy. The Holy Office replied to this question in the negative.[36]

[32] Cf. *supra*, p. 57.

[33] *De Eucharistia*, II, n. 804: "Unde necessarium est indultum apostolicum ut sacerdos consecret in alieno ritu; quod per modum actus nunquam conceditur, sed aliquando permittitur per modum habitus temporanei etiam sine transitu ad alienum ritum."

[34] Eugenius IV, const. *Exultate Deo*, 22 nov. 1439, § 12—*Fontes*, n. 52; Denzinger, *Enchiridion*, n. 698.

[35] S. C. de Prop. Fide (C. G.), 30 ian. 1635—*Fontes*, n. 4453; *Collect.*, n. 81.

[36] S. C. S. Off., 7 aug. 1704, § 2—*Fontes*, n. 770; *Collect.*, n. 267.

This precept of adding water to the wine was binding on Oriental priests as well as on Latin priests. The Code of Canon Law still includes this law of the Council of Florence in canon 814: "Sacrosanctum Missae sacrificium offerri debet ex pane et vino, cui modicissima aqua miscenda est."

The Oriental priests had another custom of long standing,[37] that of adding some hot water—*zeon*—to the Precious Blood before Communion. Pope Benedict XIV allowed the continuance of this custom in whatever Rite prescribed this practice in the celebration of the Liturgy.[38]

The Synod of Zamość (1720), on the other hand, had previously forbidden Ruthenian priests to add warm water to the chalice after the consecration:

> "Inhibet sancta Synodus gravem ob causam, et abrogat toleratam in Orientali Ecclesia consuetudinem ad consecratas calicis species, aquam tepidam effundendi post consecrationem, ante communionem." [39]

The same restriction was placed on the Maronites by the Synod of Mount Lebanon (1736). This Synod declared that although the custom of adding warm water to the chalice before the Communion was permitted by the Roman Church to Oriental Rites which had this custom, nevertheless priests of the Maronite Rite were in no way permitted to follow this practice which was still in use among the Greeks. The reasons given by the Synod for prohibiting this custom were the following: there was the danger that the addition of warm water would change the species of the wine; and the mystery which the Greeks wished to represent by the addition of warm water was fully signified and equally symbolized by the addition of water before the consecration. The warm water was added to signify the flow of blood and water from the side of Our Lord after He was pierced with a lance. But, so declared the Synod, this fact was

[37] Cf. *supra*, p. 39.

[38] Const. *Etsi pastoralis*, § VI, n. II—*Fontes*, n. 328; *Collect.*, n. 338; ep. encycl. *Allatae sunt*, § 26—*Fontes*, n. 434; *Collect.*, n. 395.

[39] Synod of Zamość (1720), tit. III, 4, a—*Fonti*, XI, 729.

equally well signified by the first infusion of water before the consecration.[40]

The practice of adding water to the Precious Blood before the Communion, although permitted by Pope Benedict XIV, seems to have been prescribed only in the Liturgy of the Greeks.[41]

[40] Synod of Mount Lebanon (1736), pars II, cap. xii, n. 7—*Coll. Lac.*, II, 195.

[41] Synod of Mount Lebanon, *loc. cit.* The Armenians never adopted the practice of adding the *zeon* to the Precious Blood. Cf. King, *Notes on the Catholic Liturgies*, p. 494.

## CHAPTER II

# MIXTURE OF RITES

THE Code of Canon Law indicates clearly that the Church does not favor a mixture of Rites. Canon 816 states that each priest must follow his own Rite in the celebration of Mass. The same prescription applies to the priest when he administers Holy Communion, for canon 851, § 1, orders the priest to distribute Holy Communion according to his own Rite, either in unleavened or in leavened bread. In these two canons the Code merely affirms what has been the mind of the Church for centuries.

Pope Pius V (1566-1572) condemned the promiscuity of Rites in unmistakable terms. He referred to it as an *abuse*.[1] Pope Clement XI (1700-1721) refused to allow Latin priests to celebrate Mass in the Greek Rite in Latin Churches. This he did in a Brief of May 9, 1705, to Cardinal Leopold Kollonitz (1631-1707), Primate of Hungary (1695-1707). The Cardinal had asked permission to allow the prolongation of the faculty given to some Latin priests to celebrate Mass in the Greek Rite temporarily, in order to preserve the faith of his people after the Turks were driven out of Hungary.[2]

Pope Benedict XIV (1740-1758) followed this same policy of restricting the interritual celebration of Mass.[3] He also forbade Holy Communion consecrated in unleavened bread to be kept in

[1] Const. *Providentia,* 20 aug. 1566, §1: " . . . propterea hunc abusum ab Ecclesia Dei extirpare et submovere volentes, omnes, et singulas licentias, et facultates huiusmodi hactenus etiam Motu proprio . . . et ex quibusvis causis quomodolibet concessas. . . . Apostolica auctoritate ex certa scientia hac praesenti nostra perpetuo valitura Constitutione revocamus, cassamus, annullamus, et irritamus. . . ."—*Fontes,* n. 113.

[2] Cf. Benedictus XIV, ep. encycl., *Alletae sunt,* 26 iul. 1755, § 34—*Fontes,* n. 434. Cf. also Nilles (*Symbolae,* I, 3-86), who wrote much on this question.

[3] Const. *Etsi pastoralis,* 26 maii, 1742, § VI, n. X; § IX, n. XV—*Fontes,* n. 328; *Collect.,* n. 338; ep. encycl. *Allatae sunt,* 26 iul. 1755, §§ 33-36—*Fontes,* n. 434; *Collect.,* n. 395.

the same tabernacle with Holy Communion consecrated in leavened bread, if there were churches of both Rites in a place, or if in the one church there were two altars each having a tabernacle.[4] Later on, however, Pope Pius IX (1846-1878) tolerated the long-standing practice of the metropolitan province of Lemberg, in accordance with which the Holy Eucharist, though consecrated in leavened and unleavened bread by the priests of the respective Rites; could be preserved in one and the same tabernacle, as long as the abuse of interritual administration was safely obviated.[5]

The prohibition which barred a priest from consecrating the Body of Our Lord and of administering Holy Communion in a Rite not his own was duly stressed by Pope Benedict XIV,[6] and later again by Pope Pius X (1903-1914). In his Constitution *Tradita ab antiquis,* Pius X stated:

> "Haec Nos igitur de Apostolicae potestatis plenitudine statuimus et sancimus:
> I. Sacris promiscuo ritu operari sacerdotibus ne liceat: propterea suae quisque Ecclesiae ritu Sacramentum Corporis Domini *conficiant* et *ministrent.*" [7]

A pronouncement of the Sacred Congregation for the Propagation of the Faith also demanded that a priest administer Holy Communion in his own Rite. In a letter to the Archbishop of Smyrna, the Sacred Congregation demanded that each priest administer the Holy Eucharist to the faithful according to his proper Rite. The Congregation then quoted § 23 of the Encyclical Letter *Allatae sunt,* which prohibited a mixture of Rite.[8]

[4] Const. *Etsi pastoralis,* § VI, n. XI—*Fontes,* n. 328; *Collect.,* n. 338.

[5] S. C. de Prop. Fide pro negotiis ritus orientalis, 25 ian. 1864—*Coll. Lac.,* II, 566 c.

[6] Ep. encycl. *Allatae sunt,* § 23: "Moneanturque impensius sacerdotes Latini, vel Graeci ritus, ne Eucharistiam consecrare, ac distribuere iuxta proprium cuiusque ritum praetermittant."—*Fontes,* n. 434; *Collect.,* n. 395. Cf. const. *Etsi pastoralis,* § I, n. II; § VI, nn. X and XI.—*Fontes,* n. 328; *Collect.,* n. 338.

[7] 14 sept. 1912, n. I—*Fontes,* n. 698.

[8] *Litt. ad Archiep. Smyrnen.,* 24 sept. 1863—*Fontes,* n. 4858; *Collect.,* n. 1242.

Thus the mind of the Church is seen as opposed to the mixture of Rites, both in the celebration of Mass and in the distribution of Holy Communion.[9] Nevertheless canon 851, § 2, admits an exception with regard to the distribution of Holy Communion, which exception will be more clearly considered in the chapter treating of the administration of Holy Communion.[10]

[9] Cf. S. C. de Prop. Fide (C. G.), 11 dec. 1838, n. 22—*Fontes*, n. 4778; *Collect.*, n. 879; also (C. G.), 12 martii 1758—*Collect.*, n. 409; and 4 sept. 1721—*Collect.*, n. 296.

[10] Cf. chapter 4, *supra*, p. 78.

## CHAPTER III

## THE CELEBRATION OF HOLY MASS

As a general rule the Oriental churches had only one altar, and upon this altar only one Mass was celebrated each day. This custom once was common in both the Eastern and the Western Churches. Although this practice has long since been relinquished in the Western Church, it was still retained and honored in the Eastern Church, so that the celebration of more than one Mass on an altar each day was forbidden, even if it served to satisfy the piety of the priests and of the faithful.[1] However, this rule was not without its exceptions. The Maronites, for example, permitted the celebration of more than one Mass a day on an altar. On the altar on which the bishop has celebrated the divine Liturgy, no other Mass may be celebrated on the same day unless permission has first been obtained.[2]

Due to the increase in the number of the clergy, the restriction regarding the use of an altar often occasioned much difficulty. The problem was solved in the Oriental Rites by means of the practice of concelebration, which was duly approved by the Holy See. It was made permissible, when there were many priests who wished to celebrate Mass, that they offer the Liturgy upon the same altar at the same time with the bishop or with some other priest. However, they were all required to wear the vestments customarily used for the celebration of the divine Liturgy, to recite the whole Liturgy, and to pronounce the words of Consecration together just as if they were celebrating the Holy Sacrifice individually.[3]

[1] Benedictus XIV, const. *Etsi pastoralis,* 26 maii 1742, § VI, n. VIII—*Fontes,* n. 328; *Collect.,* n. 338; ep. encycl. *Demandatam,* 24 dec. 1743, § 8—*Fontes,* n. 338; ep. encycl. *Allatae sunt,* 26 iulii 1755, § 37—*Fontes,* n. 434; *Collect.,* n. 395. Cf. Gasparri, *De Eucharistia,* I, n. 287.

[2] Synod of Mount Lebanon (1736), pars II, cap. xiii, n. 17: "In altari autem, in quo Episcopus missam celebravit, nullus alius sacerdos ea die celebrare praesumat, nisi prius licentiam obtinuerit."—*Coll. Lac.,* II, 222.

[3] Ep. encycl. *Demandatam,* § 9; *Allatae sunt,* § 38; Synod of Mount Lebanon, *ibid.,* n. 18. Cf. Gasparri, *ibid.,* n. 360.

The only examples of concelebration in the Latin Church occur in the ordination Mass of priests, when the newly ordained offer the Mass with the ordaining bishop, and in the Mass of the consecration of a bishop, when two other bishops assist the consecrating prelate in his act of consecrating the new bishop, and the newly consecrated bishop offers the Mass in union with the consecrating prelate.[4] These are the only two occasions on which the Code of Canon Law in canon 803 permits concelebration: "Non licet pluribus sacerdotibus concelebrare, praeterquam in Missa ordinationis presbyterorum et in Missa consecrationis Episcoporum secundum Pontificale Romanum."

Another means of facilitating matters in order that more Masses might be said each day was the building of chapels or oratories adjoining the church. These were called *parecclesiae*. Besides, there was often found in Byzantine churches not only a Greek altar for the Greek priests, but also a Latin altar for Latin priests. However, in the United States the Oriental churches have never had this altar for the Latins.[5]

Pope Benedict XIV permitted this building of additional altars in Oriental churches for Latin and for Oriental priests.[6] But the celebration of the Liturgy on the additional altars was restricted by him to Sundays and to feast-days (also secondary feast-days) falling during the week. On the ferial days of Lent, except on Saturdays and of course on Sundays, only the *Missa Praesanctificatorum* was permitted on them.[7]

Duskie states that in recent times some of the Orientals have departed from the ancient custom of permitting only one Mass on an altar each day, and now permit more than one Mass on the same altar the same day to satisfy the piety of the people. But the Holy Sacrifice is repeated by different celebrants.[8]

A Latin priest may say only one Mass a day, except on the feast

[4] Ep. encycl. *Allatae sunt,* § 38.

[5] Ep. encycl. *Allatae sunt,* §§ 39-40. Cf. Gasparri, *ibid.*, n. 287, and Duskie, *The Canonical Status of the Orientals in the United States*, pp. 114-115.

[6] Ep. encycl. *Demandatam,* § 9; const. *Etsi pastoralis,* § VI, n. IX.

[7] Ep. encycl. *Demandatam,* § 8; const. *Etsi pastoralis,* § VI, n. XVI.

[8] *Op. cit.*, p. 114.

of Christmas and on All Souls' Day. However, on days of obligation, if a considerable number of the faithful would miss Mass on account of the lack of priests, the ordinary, if he prudently judges it necessary, can permit a priest to celebrate two Masses on those days.[9] This privilege of celebrating more than one Mass a day is not given to Orientals except to those of the Byzantine Rite. Rather, when the Orientals asked the Holy See for the privilege of celebrating three Masses on Christmas, the grant of the privilege was refused.[10] And later, when again the Holy See was asked whether Orientals enjoyed the same privilege as Latin priests, namely, of celebrating three Masses on the feast of Christmas and on All Souls' Day, the reply was in the negative.[11] As stated above, in virtue of an instruction issued in 1933 by the Sacred Congregation for the Oriental Church, bination may now be permitted in the Byzantine Rite if written permission is obtained from the Holy See.[12]

The Church did not favor the indiscriminate use of a church building or of an altar of another Rite. Pope Benedict XIV strictly forbade the priests of the Latin Rite to celebrate Mass in churches of the Greek Rite and upon the main altar in these churches, except in the case of necessity, namely, when there were no churches of the Latin Rite in that place, and when there were no other altars in the church of the Greek Rite. Moreover, the Latin priest had to obtain permission from the pastor of the Greek church, who however was not free to refuse this permission under such circumstances.[13] On

[9] Canon 806.

[10] Benedictus XIV, ep. *In superiori,* 29 dec. 1755, §§ 1-2—*Fontes,* n. 437. Cf. const. *Etsi pastoralis,* § VI, n. XVI; ep. encycl. *Demandatam,* §§ 8-9.

[11] S. C. de Prop. Fide pro negotiis ritu orientalis, 22 mart. 1916—*Acta Apostolicae Sedis, Commentarium Officiale* (Romae, 1909—), VIII (1916), 104 (hereafter cited *AAS*).

[12] S. C. Or., *Instructio pro sacerdotibus Byzantini Ritus super liturgica binatione,* 1 febr. 1933: "Bis in die Sacrum celebrare nusquam licet, nisi Apostolica Sedes vel per se vel Ordinarium gravibus de causis, facultatem scripto dederit."—*AAS,* XXVI (1934), 181-182.

[13] Const. *Etsi pastoralis,* §VI, n. VIII: " . . . interdicitur autem Latinis sacerdotibus, ne Missas, et alia divina officia in dictis Graecorum ecclesiis, et super eorum altaribus maioribus, extra casum alicuius necessitatis, et aliorum altarium ecclesiarumque defectus, et nisi ex parochi Graeci consensu, quem

the other hand, the priests of the Greek Rite were forbidden to celebrate the Liturgy in churches of the Latin Rite unless they had obtained permission from the Latin ordinary, or from his vicar general, who could grant this permission even though no necessity existed as long as some spiritual good could be expected from this celebration.[14]

Pope Benedict XIV also stated that this celebration of the Divine Sacrifice in a church of another Rite did not constitute a promiscuity of Rites. Even though there were churches of their own Rite in Rome, Armenian, Coptic, Melkite and Greek priests celebrated the Liturgy in Latin churches in order to satisfy their devotion. The Pope did not condemn this practice, but only required that they have all the things necessary to celebrate the Liturgy in their own Rite.[15]

It was understood that a priest who celebrated Mass in a church of another Rite or upon an altar of another Rite had to perform the Holy Sacrifice according to the rubrics of his own Rite. Generally, the use of the vestments and of the sacred vessels, as well as of the altar, was reserved to a Rite and could not be used by priests of another Rite. But Pope Benedict XIV confirmed the privilege granted by Pope Clement VIII in the year 1602 by which Ruthenian

nullatenus huiusmodi in casibus negare possit, celebrent."—*Fontes*, n. 328. Cf. also *ibid.*, § IX, n. XV, and ep. encycl. *Allatae sunt*, § 36—*Fontes*, n. 434.

[14] Const. *Etsi pastoralis*, § IX, n. XVI: "Nec presbyteri, et clerici Graeci in ecclesiis Latinorum, inconsulto Episcopo, cui illae subiiciuntur, vel eius spiritualibus Vicario Generali, Missas, et alia divina officia cum solemnitatibus, et cantu celebrent. Ut autem praefatus Episcopus, sive Vicarius Generalis, praefatam licentiam rite concedere valeant, nulla praecisa necessitas pro causa requiritur, sed satis est, ut aliqua spiritualis utilitas inde speretur."—*Fontes*, n. 328. Cf. ep. encycl. *Allatae sunt*, § 35—*Fontes*, n. 434 and const. *Imposito nobis*, 29 mart. 1751, § 7, where Pope Clement VIII is quoted.—*Fontes*, n. 410.

[15] Ep. encycl. *Allatae sunt*, § 35: " . . . Verum, uti iam diximus, interdicta ritus permixtio appellari nunquam poterit, si ob legitimam aliquam causam sacerdos Orientalis Ritus ab Apostolica Sede probati, in Latinorum Ecclesiam admittatur, ut ibi Missam, caeterasque functiones celebret, et sacramenta populo nationis suae administret. Id palam Romae fieri intuemur, ubi sacerdotibus Armenis, Cophtis, Melchitis, et Graecis patent ad Missam celebrandam templa nostra, ut illorum pietati satisfiat; quamvis suas peculiares ecclesias habeant, ubi rem divinam facere possent; dummodo tamen sacra indumenta, et caetera, quae ad Missae celebrationem iuxta ipsorum ritu necessaria sunt, . . ."—*Fontes*, n. 434.

priests were permitted, in the case of necessity and even for the sake of devotion, to celebrate the Liturgy according to the Ruthenian Rite in churches and upon altars and with the sacred vessels and vestments of the Latin Rite. And, on the other hand, the Latin priests were permitted to celebrate Mass in the Latin Rite on the altars in the Ruthenian churches, and to use the sacred vessels and vestments of the Ruthenian Rite.[16]

A similar privilege was granted to the priests of the Armenian Rite by Pope Gregory XVI (1831-1846) who allowed them in the case of urgent necessity and when they lacked vestments of their own Rite to celebrate the Liturgy in churches of the Latin Rite and to wear the vestments of the Latin Rite.[17]

The Code of Canon Law abrogated the former legislation regarding the prohibited celebration of Mass in a church of another Rite and upon an altar of another Rite. Canon 823, § 2, states the law which now obtains for priests of both the Latin Rite and of the Oriental Rites:

> "Deficiente altari proprii ritus, sacerdote fas est ritu proprio celebrare in altari consecrato alius ritus catholici, non autem super Graecorum Antimensiis."

Four conditions must be fulfilled, according to canon 823, § 2, in order that a priest may licitly celebrate Mass on an altar of another Rite: (1) that there be no altar of the priest's own Rite available; (2) that the priest celebrate Mass according to his own Rite; (3) that the altar be consecrated; and (4) that the altar pertain to a Catholic Rite. A priest would sin gravely if he celebrated Mass on

[16] Pope Clement VIII as quoted by Pope Benedict XIV, const. *Imposito nobis,* 29 mart. 1751, § 7: "Sacerdotes Rutheni non schismatici in ecclesiis catholicorum ritus latini, altaribus, calicibus, et vestibus sacris eorundem catholicorum uti, et Missam celebrare possint, in casu necessitatis, ac etiam solum devotionis causa, dummodo ritu rutheno celebrent. Et e contra sacerdotes ritus latini in ecclesiis ruthenorum non schismaticorum, altaribus, et calicibus, ac vestibus sacris uti et Missam celebrare valeant, ritu tamen latino. Et praedicta serventur secluso omni scandalo, et de licentia praelatorum, et rectorum ipsarum ecclesiarum."—*Fontes,* n. 410.

[17] Gregorius XVI, ep. encycl. *Inter gravissimas,* 3 febr. 1832, § 6—*Fontes,* n. 483.

an altar of another Rite and even one of these conditions were unfulfilled.[18] This canon, then, does not prohibit the celebration of Mass in a church building of another Rite, but only the use of an altar of another Rite without any necessity. In such a case, however, the sole permission that a priest needs in order to celebrate Mass in a church and upon an altar of another Rite must be obtained from the pastor of the church.

In the Latin Rite there are two types of altars: (1) the immovable or fixed altar, which is a permanent structure of stone, consisting of the table upon which the Holy Sacrifice is offered and the support or base consecrated together as one whole; (2) the movable or portable altar, which consists of a solid piece of natural stone, generally of small size, which alone is consecrated; or the same stone with its support, which, however, was not consecrated together with the table as one whole.[19] Before the Sacrifice of the Mass can be celebrated on an altar, whether it be a fixed altar or a portable altar-stone, the altar must be consecrated according to the form prescribed by the Roman Pontifical.[20]

The Byzantine Rite also distinguishes two types of altars: (1) altars consecrated by a bishop, which are found only in consecrated churches, and are the same as the consecrated altars of the Latin Rite; (2) the *Antimension,* which is used for the celebration of the Liturgy on a consecrated altar as well as on an unconsecrated altar, and which corresponds to the corporal and altar-stone of the Latin Rite.[21]

Since a priest of the Latin Rite must celebrate Mass on a consecrated altar-stone, he can use the Greek *Antimension* only if he

18 Cappello, *De Sacramentis,* I, n. 720.

19 Canon 1197, §§ 1 and 2, as translated by Harold E. Collins (*The Church Edifice and Its Appointments,* Philadelphia: The Dolphin Press, 1936, p. 43).

20 Canon 1199, § 1.

21 Cf. Stephen C. Gulovich, "Mass and Communion According to the Oriental Rite in a Church of the Latin Rite," *The Jurist* (Washington, D. C.: published by the School of Canon Law, the Catholic University of America, 1941—), II (1942), 48.

has an apostolic indult to do so.[22] The indult to use the Greek *Antimension* is given to priests who enroll in the Catholic Near East Welfare Association. To these priests is granted the privilege of celebrating Mass in churches of the Byzantine Rite on the Greek corporal (*super antimensiis Graecorum*). This privilege was given at Rome on January 28, 1928.[23] However, there is nothing in this indult which could lead one to conclude that the implied requirement of canon 823, § 2, is abrogated. A priest who has this privilege granted to him by the Catholic Near East Welfare Association can celebrate Mass on the *Antimension* only when the condition stated in the first part of canon 823, § 2, is fulfilled. Accordingly, the priest can celebrate Mass on the *Antimension* only when it is impossible for him to offer the Holy Sacrifice on a consecrated altar of his own Rite, whether portable or fixed, or upon an altar consecrated in another Rite, whether portable or fixed. Permission was likewise granted to military chaplains serving at the front to offer Mass without an altar-stone. This permission made it possible for them to use an *Antimension* instead.[24]

A priest of the Latin Rite who has the privilege of the portable altar can celebrate Mass, using his own altar-stone, in an Oriental Church, but he is not obliged to do so. He can celebrate Mass in an Oriental Church upon his own altar-stone, since canon 823, § 2, requires only that a priest celebrate Mass on an altar of his own Rite, and not that he must offer the Holy Sacrifice in a church of his own Rite. But the Latin priest would not be obliged to say Mass in a church of the Oriental Rite, for the privilege of a portable altar carries with it the faculty of celebrating Mass in any place,

[22] Canon 823, § 2. Cf. const. *Etsi pastoralis*, § VI, n. XIX—*Fontes*, n. 328; *Collect.*, n. 338; const. *Imposito nobis*, 29 mart. 1751, §§ 1, 6-8— *Fontes*, n. 410.

[23] No other record mentioning this indult could be found except the leaflet issued by the Catholic Near East Welfare Association, which lists the indulgences, faculties and privileges enjoyed by the members of this Association. The privilege to use the Greek *Antimension* is listed along with other privileges.

[24] "Decrees and Decisions," *The Jurist*, III (1943), 158. Cf. Bouscaren, *The Canon Law Digest* (2 vols., Milwaukee: The Bruce Publishing Co., Vol. I, 1934, Vol. II, 1943), II, 204.

provided that it be respectable and decent; only celebration at sea is excluded.[25]

When a priest of some Oriental Rite in the lack of an altar of his own Rite celebrates the Liturgy in a church of the Latin Rite, he can use any Latin altar which is consecrated, whether fixed or portable. Like a Latin priest, an Oriental priest must also obtain permission from the pastor of the Latin Church, and he must celebrate the Liturgy according to his own Rite. The licit celebration demands also that the Oriental priest use the sacred vessels and vestments that are proper to his own Rite, with the exception of the Ruthenian and Armenian priests who can use the sacred vessels and vestments of the Latin Rite if they do not have those of their own Rite.[26]

A priest of the Byzantine Rite must always use an *Antimension* when he celebrates the divine Liturgy, regardless of the fact that the altar is or is not consecrated.[27] Since the *Antimension* is an altar of the Byzantine Rite, a priest of that Rite can celebrate the Liturgy in a church of the Latin Rite, even though there are churches of his own Rite available. He would not violate the law of canon 823, § 2, for he would be offering the Holy Sacrifice upon an altar of his own Rite. He would have to obtain permission from the pastor of the Latin church, and would have to celebrate according to the rubrics of his own Rite and use, unless he were a Ruthenian priest, his own vestments and sacred vessels.

It has been said that a priest who wishes to say Mass in a Church and upon an altar of another Rite acting under the circumstances

25 Canon 822, § 3.

26 Const. *Imposito nobis*, § 7—*Fontes*, n. 410; ep. encycl. *Inter gravissimas*, 3 febr. 1832, § 6—*Fontes*, n. 483.

27 Renaudot, I, 311: "Graeci quoque non celebrant vulgo, etiam in solidis altaribus, absque Antimensiis quod in Orientalibus non observatum huc usque a nobis est." Cf. I, 164-165. Cf. also const. *Etsi pastoralis*, § VI, nn. XVII-XVIII —*Fontes*, n. 328; const. *Imposito nobis*, § 4—*Fontes*, n. 410; Nilles, *Symbolae*, II, 861, ftn. 1. Among the Rites which belong to the Byzantine discipline are the Greek, the Ruthenian, the Ukrainian, the Italo-Greek, the Hungarian Oriental, the Melkite, the Georgian Catholic, the Rumanian, the Bulgarian, the Serbian and the Russian Catholics.

as required by canon 823, § 2, must have the permission of the pastor of the church in which he wants to celebrate Mass. Canon 804, § 1, states that a priest who desires to say Mass in a church other than that to which he is assigned upon showing to the pastor or the rector of the church authentic and valid letters of recommendation, commonly called the celebret, must be permitted to celebrate Mass.

> Canon 804.—§ 1. "Sacerdos extraneus ecclesiae in qua celebrare postulat, exhibens authenticas et adhuc validas litteras commendatitias sui Ordinarii, si sit saecularis, vel sui Superioris, si religiosus, vel Sacrae Congregationis pro Ecclesia Orientali, si sit ritus orientalis, ad Missae celebrationem admittatur, nisi interim aliquid eum commisisse constet, cur a Missae celebratione repelli debeat."

The celebret gives testimony of the bearer's rank and certifies that he is free from ecclesiastical censure; it is also a testimonial of the priest's good standing in his diocese.[28] The celebret must be authentic, that is, it must be signed by the proper authority and have the official seal attached to it.[29] Besides being authentic, the celebret must still be valid. Canon 804, § 1, does not state for how long the celebret remains valid after it is given, but the period of validity should be determined by the ordinary who issues the document. When this period has elapsed, the celebret no longer has any value. The celebret can also become invalid should the bearer render himself unworthy to celebrate Mass. But a pastor or rector could not refuse permission to a priest to celebrate Mass in his church by declaring the celebret invalid in consequence of any confessional knowledge concerning the priest.[30]

A priest of the Latin Rite must obtain the celebret from his ordinary if he is a secular priest, or from his superior if he is a religious. A priest of an Oriental Rite must obtain his celebret from

[28] Wernz, *Ius Decretalium,* III, n. 532.

[29] Augustine, *A Commentary on the New Code of Canon Law,* IV (3. ed., 1925), 131.

[30] Decr. S. Off., 18 nov. 1682—Denzinger, *Enchiridion,* n. 1220. Cf. Augustine, *loc. cit.*, and Duskie, *The Canonical Status of the Orientals in the United States,* p. 102.

the Sacred Oriental Congregation. This celebret from the Sacred Oriental Congregation is necessary for priests who come to this country to collect alms or to ask for Mass stipends,[81] and for those who come for some other reason, economic or moral, or simply for a visit.[82]

The Sacred Oriental Congregation issued a decree, *Qua sollerti*, for priests of the Oriental Rites who come to the United States to administer to the spiritual needs of the faithful of their own Rite. A priest of an Oriental Rite who is sent to the United States for this purpose must be approved by the Sacred Oriental Congregation, and must also receive from the same Congregation testimonial letters, commonly called a celebret, which shall be valid for the purpose stated, and for the time required for the journey. In order to avoid all doubt or difficulty on the part of the bishops of this country, the Sacred Congregation will send notice to the ordinary of the diocese where the priest of the Oriental Rite intends to establish his domicile, through the Apostolic Delegate or, if the matter is urgent, directly to the ordinary, giving notice at the same time to the Apostolic Delegate. When the priest arrives at his designated diocese, he shall present himself to the local ordinary and show him the testimonial letters which he has from the Sacred Oriental Congregation and the discessorial letters from his own bishop. The local ordinary shall give the priest permission to celebrate Mass or the divine Liturgy, and to perform all the other priestly offices for the spiritual care of the faithful of his own Rite. The priest shall be subject to the ordinary of that place where he has established his domicile, and must obey all the orders of the local ordinary, whether he be an ordinary of his own Rite or of the Latin Rite.[83]

Since the celebret which the priest obtained from the Sacred

[81] S. C. Or., decr. *Saepenumero*, 7 ian. 1930—*AAS*, XXII (1930), 108-110; Bouscaren, *The Canon Law Digest*, I, 27-29.

[82] S. C. Or., *Non raro*, 7 ian. 1930—*AAS*, XXII (1930), 106-108; Bouscaren, *ibid.*, 24-26.

[83] S. C. Or., decr. *Qua sollerti*, 23 dec. 1929, §§ 5-12—*AAS*, XXII (1930), 102-104; Bouscaren, *ibid.*, 20-22.

Oriental Congregation is valid only for the time required to make the journey to his new diocese, and since the priest becomes subject to the local ordinary when he arrives at his destination and receives from the ordinary permission to celebrate the divine Liturgy and to perform all the other priestly offices, it is correct to assume, then, that thereafter the local ordinary (whether of the Latin Rite or of an Oriental Rite) is the proper authority to issue the celebret to an Oriental priest in order that he may celebrate the Liturgy outside his own church.

When a priest wishes to celebrate Mass in a church other than that to which he is attached, he should show a celebret issued by the proper authority to the priest in charge of the church. If the visiting priest has no celebret, but is known by the rector of the church to be a priest in good standing, he may be allowed to say Mass. If, however, he is unknown to the rector, he may nevertheless be permitted to say Mass once or twice, provided that he wears the ecclesiastical garb, does not receive any remuneration under any title from that church for the celebration of Mass, and enters his name, office and diocese in a book to be specially kept for that purpose.[84]

From what has been said, then, it is to be noted: (1) that a priest of the Latin Rite must obtain the celebret from his ordinary, if he is a secular, or from his superior, if he is a religious; (2) that a priest of an Oriental Rite who has his proper ordinary in this country must receive the celebret from him; (3) that a priest of an Oriental Rite who is subject to the jurisdiction of a local Latin ordinary must obtain the celebret from the Latin ordinary in whose diocese he has established his domicile for the purpose of administering to the spiritual needs of the faithful of his own Rite; (4) that a priest of an Oriental Rite who is merely visiting in this country, or has come for some purpose other than to administer to the faithful of his own Rite and so is subject to no ordinary in the United States, must bring with him his celebret and his credentials obtained from the Sacred Oriental Congregation; and (5) that even the priest of an Oriental Rite who comes to this country to care for

[84] Canon 804, § 2, as translated by Woywod (*A Practical Commentary on the Code of Canon Law*, I, 373).

souls must have this celebret for presentation on his arrival to the ordinary to whom he is to be subject.[35]

[35] The following is a copy of a document testifying to a priest's good standing which was issued by the Exarch of the Philadelphia diocese of the Byzantine-Slavonic Rite:

Bishop's Chancery Office

SEAL

815 North Franklin Street
Philadelphia, Pa.
Date

No. ........................................

To Whom It May Concern:

This is to certify that the Rev. N.N. ............................................................ is hereby appointed by me, as Bishop of the Ruthenian (Ukrainian) Greek Catholic Diocese, pastor (assistant pastor) of ........................................................ Church in ........................................................ and as such he is duly authorized and empowered to celebrate the Holy Mass and administer the Sacraments to the Ruthenian (Ukrainian) Greek Catholic Faithful in the said cities.

✠ Constantine Bohachevsky,
Bishop.

## CHAPTER IV

## THE ADMINISTRATION OF HOLY COMMUNION

THE Council of Constance (1414-1418) had restricted in favor of the celebrant the reception of the Holy Eucharist in both species, and it declared that the laity of the Latin Rite should receive Holy Communion solely under the species of bread.[1] The Council of Trent (1545-1563) defined that the laity and the non-celebrating clergy were not obliged by any divine precept to receive Holy Communion in both species, and that Holy Communion under one species was sufficient for salvation. This Council not only approved the custom of communicating under one species, but also decreed it as binding under the precept of the common law, which could not be changed except by the authority of the Church.[2] This law was enacted for the Western Church. On their reunion with Rome the Eastern Churches who wished to retain the practice of distributing Holy Communion to the faithful under the form of bread and wine were permitted to do so.[3]

The Maronite Synod of Mount Lebanon legislated that Holy Communion was to be administered to the laity and to clerics in Minor Orders under the one species of bread. A priest who dared to administer Holy Communion in both species was to be punished by a personal interdict.[4] The old custom of placing the Eucharist in the hands of men and on a cloth held by the women was declared to be no longer acceptable in the Maronite Church. The custom of the Roman Church had to be followed, that of communicating in one species, and priests were forbidden to place the Holy Eucharist in the hands of the communicants, but were commanded to place It

[1] Denzinger, *Enchiridion*, n. 626; Hardouin, VIII, 381 B; Mansi, XXVII, 727 C.

[2] Sess. XXI, *de Communione sub utraque specie, et parvulorum*, cc. 1 et 2—Denzinger, *op. cit.*, nn. 930-931.

[3] Benedictus XIV, const. *Etsi pastoralis*, 26 maii. 1742, § VI, n. XV—*Fontes*, 4. 328; *Collect.*, n. 338.

[4] Synodus Montis Libani (1736), pars II, cap. XII, n. 21—*Coll. Lac.*, II, 207.

upon their tongues. The deacon had the right to receive the Precious Blood; the lower clerics could receive It only with the express permission of the Patriarch. All had to communicate in church, except in case of necessity. Only bishops could take the Eucharist from church and retain It in a decent place in their homes.[5]

Besides the Maronites, the Malabars and the Armenians (although for these Communion under both kinds is still permitted in theory) also administer Holy Communion under the one species of bread. The Copts distribute the Holy Eucharist under both species when Holy Communion is administered during the celebration of the Liturgy; outside the celebration of the Liturgy the Copts administer Holy Communion under the one species of bread.

After the Councils of Constance, of Florence and of Trent, the question of receiving Holy Communion in the form of bread alone or in both species was settled. The problem that presented itself after that was the one which dealt with the Rite which was to be followed in the administering and receiving of Holy Communion.

A rather broad concession had been granted in 1866 by the Sacred Congregation for the Propagation of the Faith when it was asked whether a Maronite or an Armenian priest (who used unleavened bread) could administer the Sacrament of the Holy Eucharist when it was consecrated according to the Latin Rite, and vice versa. The Sacred Congregation replied in the affirmative, provided that the priest used the language and ceremonies of his own Rite, and provided that in the case of the Armenians this permission was used only in those places where the custom of communicating in one species alone was observed.[6]

However, in 1893 the same Congregation for the Propagation of the Faith had refused to grant a similar concession to the Melkites in a reply to the doubts proposed by the Archbishop of Paris. Some priests of the Latin Rite celebrated Mass in the Greek-Melchite Church of Saint Julian, and then placed in the tabernacle there the hosts which they had consecrated in unleavened bread for the Com-

[5] Synodus Montis Libani, *ibid.*, n. 11—*op. cit.*, II, 199-200.

[6] S. C. de Prop. Fide (C. G.), 30 apr. 1866, ad 2am—*Fontes*, n. 4864; *Collect.*, n. 1288.

munion of the faithful. At times also a Melkite priest went to another church in the city to celebrate the Liturgy at the altar where the Blessed Sacrament was reserved. The questions proposed were whether the Melkite priest could distribute Holy Communion to the faithful of the Latin Rite with the hosts consecrated in unleavened bread, either during his Mass, or before or after his Mass. The Sacred Congregation replied in the negative to both points of doubt, so that such a distribution was not permitted unless a special faculty had been obtained from the Holy See.[7]

The reason for the divergence in the regulation of these cases seems based on the fact that the Maronites and Armenians used unleavened bread, the same as the Latins. Hence it was permitted to them to administer Holy Communion when It was consecrated in another Rite, namely the Latin, since the Holy Eucharist had been consecrated in unleavened bread. The Melkites, on the other hand, used leavened bread; that is why the Sacred Congregation refused permission to the Melkite priest to administer Holy Communion when It was consecrated in another Rite, namely in another form of bread which differed from the form of bread as used according to the Melkite Rite.

The decrees of the Sacred Congregations always refused permission to priests to administer Holy Communion consecrated in another Rite when the Holy Eucharist was consecrated in another form of bread which differed from the form of bread used in their respective Rites. The Sacred Congregation of the Holy Office was asked whether missionaries of the Latin Rite could distribute Holy Communion to the Catholics of the Greek Rite in unleavened bread, or whether the people were to be ordered to communicate in leavened bread. To this question the Congregation replied that nothing new should be inaugurated, and the mind of the Church was that missionaries had to insist that the faithful of the Greek Rite were to receive Holy Communion consecrated in leavened bread according to their own Rite and from a priest of their own Rite.[8] The same

[7] S. C. de Prop. Fide, 31 aug. 1891, as cited in Gasparri, *De Eucharistia,* II, n. 1094.

[8] S. C. S. Off., decr., 4 sept. 1721—*Collect.,* n. 296.

rule was given several times by the Sacred Congregation for the Propagation of the Faith. Missionaries of the Latin Rite were not to administer the Sacraments to Catholics of the Oriental Rites when there was a priest of their own Rite present who could do so without difficulty. Each priest had to administer the Holy Eucharist to the faithful according to his own proper Rite. A Latin priest or an Oriental priest could administer the Sacrament of Holy Viaticum in the case of necessity to persons of a different Rite, but they had to observe their own Rite in the administration.[9]

In a letter to the Archbishop of Smyrna,[10] the Sacred Congregation for the Propagation of the Faith quoted paragraph 23 of the Encyclical Letter *Allatae sunt* of Pope Benedict XIV. This Encyclical Letter warned priests of the Latin Rite and of the Greek Rite that they were to consecrate and distribute the Holy Eucharist according to their own Rite. And in paragraph 34 of the same Letter, the Pope forbade all mixture of Rites. The Latin priests were not to consecrate the Holy Eucharist in leavened bread, and then administer Holy Communion thus consecrated in leavened bread to Catholics of the Latin Rite. And in like manner, priests of Oriental Rites (who consecrated in leavened bread) were forbidden to consecrate the Holy Eucharist in unleavened bread, and then distribute Holy Communion thus consecrated in unleavened bread to the faithful.[11] Pope Benedict XIV had ruled before in his Constitution *Etsi pastoralis* that each priest had to distribute the Holy Eucharist to the faithful in his own Rite, whether Greek or Latin.[12]

The Constitution *Tradita ab antiquis* of Pope Pius X shows the tendency of the Church to be more liberal in granting permission to administer Holy Communion which was consecrated in another Rite and in a form of bread different from the form of bread used in the

[9] S. C. de Prop. Fide, litt. 11 oct. 1780—*Fontes*, n. 4584; S. C. de Prop. Fide, litt. ad Archiep. Smyrnen., 24 sept. 1863—*Fontes*, n. 4858; *Collect.*, n. 1242; Decr. 6 oct. 1863—*Coll. Lac.*, II, 564 b (art. C, § d); *Fontes*, n. 4859; *Collect.*, n. 1243.

[10] S. C. de Prop. Fide, litt. ad Archiep. Smyrnen., 24 sept. 1863—*Fontes*, n. 4858; *Collect.*, n. 1242.

[11] Ep. encycl. *Allatae sunt*, 26 iul. 1755, §§ 23 and 34—*Fontes*, n. 434.

[12] 25 maii 1742, § VI, n. XI—*Fontes*, n. 328.

Rite of the administering priest. Previous pronouncements of the Holy See had forbidden priests to distribute to the faithful the Holy Eucharist which had been consecrated according to another Rite and in a form of bread which differed from the form of bread used in their Rites. In this Constitution Pope Pius X allowed Oriental priests who used leavened bread to administer the Holy Eucharist which was consecrated in unleavened bread when there was a case of necessity. Likewise in a case of necessity a priest of the Latin Rite, or of an Oriental Rite which uses unleavened bread, could distribute Holy Communion which was consecrated in leavened bread. But the Pope added that each priest had to observe the rules of his own Rite in distributing Holy Communion.[13]

The Code of Canon Law in canon 851, § 1, has now settled the question regarding the administering of Holy Communion by commanding every priest to distribute the Holy Eucharist according to his proper Rite.

> § 1. "Sacerdos sacram communionem distribuat azymo pane vel fermentato, secundum proprium ritum."

Canon 851, § 1, states the law, which binds all priests of every Rite, Oriental as well as Latin, that they are to distribute Holy Communion consecrated in leavened bread or in unleavened bread, each one according to his own Rite. There is to be no unnecessary mixture of Rites.

However, canon 851, § 2, states an exception to § 1, and grants a concession to priests to distribute the Holy Eucharist which was consecrated in another Rite in a form of bread which is different from the form of bread used in their own Rite.

> § 2. "Ubi vero necessitas urgeat nec sacerdos diversi ritus adsit, licet sacerdoti orientali qui fermentato utitur, ministrare Eucharistiam in azymo, vicissim latino aut orientali quo utitur azymo,

[13] 14 sept. 1912, n. II—*Fontes*, n. 698. A Latin priest who in the case of necessity administered the Holy Eucharist in both species therefore used the customary formula: "Corpus Domini nostri Jesu Christi custodiat animam tuam in vitam aeternam. Amen." He did not use any adapted formula such as, for example, the following: "Corpus et Sanguis Domini nostri Jesu Christi custodiant animam tuam in vitam aeternam. Amen."

ministrare in fermentato; at suum quisque ritum ministrandi servare debet."

This paragraph of the canon is taken almost word for word from the Constitution *Tradita ab antiquis* of Pope Pius X.[14]

The decree *Cum Episcopo,* and also the decree *Cum data fuerit,* issued for the Greek-Ruthenians in the United States, contain the same law as canon 851, § 2, although the decrees do not state the law word for word as it appears in the canon.[15]

Canon 851, § 2, does not speak of the Rite in which the bread was consecrated but rather speaks of the type of bread (leavened or unleavened) used in consecration. The canon makes a distinction between Oriental priests who use leavened bread and Latin and Oriental priests who used unleavened bread. But there is no distinction made between priests of the different Oriental Rites which use leavened bread, or between Latin priests and priests of the Oriental Rites who use unleavened bread. Therefore, Duskie rightly notes that "Latin and Oriental priests who consecrate with unleavened bread, are not restricted by canon 851, § 2, to administer the Holy Eucharist consecrated according to another Rite, so long as the form of bread for the Sacrament remains the same. Likewise, the Oriental priests who use leavened bread are not prohibited to administer the Holy Eucharist consecrated according to another Oriental Rite which also uses leavened bread."[16]

There are certain conditions that must be verified before a priest can make use of the concession expressed in canon 851, § 2. The conditions demanded by this canon in order that a priest may avail himself of the privilege which it gives are: (1) that there be a case of necessity; (2) that there be no priest of the respective Rite present; (3) that each priest observe the rubrics of his own Rite when he distributes Holy Communion which was consecrated in a form of bread proper to another Rite and not proper to his own.

[14] 14 sept. 1912, n. II—*Fontes,* n. 698.

[15] S. C. de Prop. Fide pro negotiis ritus orientalis, decr. *Cum Episcopo,* 18 aug. 1914, art. 23—*AAS,* VI (1914), 462. S. C. Or., decr. *Cum data fuerit,* 1 mart. 1929, art. 32—*AAS,* XXI (1929), 158; Bouscaren, *The Canon Law Digest,* I, 14.

[16] *The Canonical Status of the Orientals in the United States,* p. 118.

The import of the second and third conditions is evident, and needs no explanation. But what constitutes a case of necessity which will make it lawful for a priest to administer Holy Communion when It was consecrated in a form of bread that is not proper to his Rite? A case of extreme necessity such as is present when a person is in danger of death would certainly justify a priest to make use of the concession granted by canon 851, § 2. But this case of necessity which urges in danger of death cannot be the only instance implied in this canon. If a priest can consecrate bread that is proper to another Rite in the case of necessity for the purpose of administering Holy Viaticum to the dying,[17] *a fortiori* he can distribute Holy Communion which was consecrated in bread that is proper to another Rite.

Canon 851, § 2, does not demand that the case of necessity be one of danger of death if a priest is to use the concession granted by it. There are other cases of necessity which would warrant its application, and which would permit a priest to administer Holy Communion when It was consecrated in bread that is proper to another Rite. But the circumstances of the case of necessity must be such that it is very important for a person to receive Holy Communion that day.[18]

A case of this kind could exist, for example, if a person of a Rite in which the Holy Eucharist is consecrated in unleavened bread were about to take a long journey during which it would be impossible for him to receive the Holy Eucharist for a long time. If it would not be possible for him before his departure on this journey to receive Holy Communion consecrated in unleavened bread except from a priest of an Oriental Rite who in his proper Rite uses leavened bread, then the priest of the Oriental Rite could lawfully administer to him Holy Communion which was consecrated in unleavened bread, provided that no priest of his own Rite be present, and the Oriental priest be not able to administer to him the Holy Eucharist which was consecrated in leavened bread.

Or it may be supposed that a person of an Oriental Rite in which the Holy Eucharist is consecrated in leavened bread is about to

[17] Cf. *supra*. pp. 58-59.

[18] Woywod, *A Practical Commentary on the Code of Canon Law*, I, n. 748.

undergo a surgical operation.[19] A short time before he is to submit to this operation he receives a visit from his pastor and expresses to him the desire to receive Holy Communion. It is found that the chaplain of the hospital, who belongs to a Rite in which the Holy Eucharist is consecrated in unleavened bread, is not available in time for administering Holy Communion to him. The pastor can then take advantage of canon 851, § 2, and administer Holy Communion though it was consecrated in unleavened bread.[20]

The same solution can also be suggested, namely that a priest may administer the Holy Eucharist consecrated in bread that is proper to another Rite, when a long interval of time has elapsed since a person last received the Holy Eucharist, or when it is necessary for him to fulfill his Easter duty.[21]

Duskie is of the opinion that if a number of devotional communicants in a Latin Church will be unable to receive Holy Communion that day because the priest in charge is attending a sick call, then a priest of an Oriental Rite, even though he consecrates in leavened bread, can distribute to the waiting congregation the Holy Eucharist which was consecrated in the Latin Rite.[22] He states as his reason for this opinion the fact that canon 863 urges the faithful to a frequent reception of the Holy Eucharist.[23] This reason

[19] The danger of death does not accompany every surgical operation in such a manner as to permit the administration of Holy Viaticum. There are many operations which ordinarily do not place the patient in danger of death. Each case must be judged individually, with due consideration of the age and the physical condition of the patient, the advances of modern surgery, and the circumstances under which the operation is to be performed.

[20] Duskie, *The Canonical Status of the Orientals in the United States*, p. 118.

[21] Cf. Duskie, *loc. cit.*; Woywod, *loc. cit.*

[22] Vermeersch-Creusen (*Epitome Iuris Canonici* [3 vols., Mechliniae-Romae: H. Dessain, Vol. II, 6. ed., 1940], n. 115), Jone (*Gesetzbuch des kanonischen Rechtes* [3 vols., Paderborn: Ferdinand Schoeningh, 1939-1940. Vol. II, 1940], 89) and Blat (*Commentarium Textus Codicis Iuris Canonici* [5 vols. in 6, Romae: ex Typographia Pontificia in Instituto Pii IX, Vol. III, Pars I, *De Sacramentis*, 1920], 179) also hold the opinion that if a person would otherwise have to forego receiving Holy Communion out of devotion, then a priest may administer the Blessed Sacrament consecrated according to another Rite.

[23] *The Canonical Status of the Orientals in the United States*, p. 119.

seems not sufficiently serious to warrant the use of the concession granted by canon 851, § 2. Duskie himself demands a serious reason and says: "Since the words of the canon stress the element of necessity, it must be the mind of the legislator to prevent indiscriminate mixing of Rites. Hence, it is proper to demand a serious reason to make use of the privilege." [24] Besides, canon 863 does not command the faithful to receive Holy Communion frequently, but merely counsels a frequent reception of the Holy Eucharist, and hence does not oblige under penalty of sin. Canon 851, § 1, on the other hand, is a precept which binds priests both of the Latin Rite and of the Oriental Rites under pain of sin. Furthermore, according to the opinion expressed by Duskie canon 851, § 2, appears to lose its force to such an extent that it could just as well have omitted the words *"ubi vero necessitas urgeat,"* since there would scarcely be a case which in the light of its accompanying circumstances could not be thought to warrant the use of the conclusion made in the canon and thus the law enacted in canon 851, § 2, would indeed be useless.[25]

A priest could be face to face with circumstances when he wonders if he may use the privilege granted by canon 851, § 2. Such a case could exist when a priest of an Oriental Rite in which leavened bread is used for consecration attends Holy Mass celebrated by a Latin priest, who must use unleavened bread for consecrating the Holy Eucharist. When the time comes for distributing Holy Communion to the faithful, there is such a large number of communicants that the priest of the Oriental Rite wonders whether he could help the celebrant with the distribution of Holy Communion in order to lighten the task of the Latin priest and to shorten the delay in the completion of the Mass.

Canon 851, § 2, postulates as one of the conditions that "a priest of the Rite be not present" before a priest of another Rite can make use of the privilege which it allows. The Latin priest is present, and there is no necessity urging the Oriental priest to help in

[24] *Loc. cit.*

[25] Cf. Woywod, *A Practical Commentary on the Code of Canon Law,* I, n. 748.

the distribution of Holy Communion. The reasons which would influence the priest of the Oriental Rite in this case do not warrant his use of the concession granted by canon 851, § 2.

However, if the priest who attends the Mass belongs to the Armenian Rite (or to one of the other Rites which use unleavened bread, namely, the Maronite, the Chaldean, the Syro-Malabar or the Italo-Greek), then the priest of the Armenian Rite (or of the other Rites mentioned) could assist the Latin priest in the distribution of Holy Communion to the faithful. The reason why the priest of the Armenian Rite (or of the other Rites mentioned) can help the Latin priest is that the priests of both the Armenian Rite and of the Latin Rite consecrate the Holy Eucharist in unleavened bread and distribute Holy Communion thus consecrated in unleavened bread to the faithful. This is in accordance with canon 851, § 2, which makes no distinction between Latin priests and priests of the Oriental Rites who use unleavened bread, as was noted before.[26]

The law as expressed in the Constitution *Tradita ab antiquis* of Pope Pius X, in the decrees *Cum Episcopo* and *Cum data fuerit,* and in canon 851, § 2, insists that the priest must observe the rubrics of his own Rite when he distributes Holy Communion which was consecrated in a form of bread proper to another Rite but not proper to his own.[27]

[26] Cf. *supra,* p. 83.

[27] Const. *Tradita ab antiquis,* 14 sept. 1912, n. II—*Fontes,* n. 698; decr. *Cum Episcopo,* 18 aug. 1914, art. 23—*AAS,* VI (1914), 462; decr. *Cum data fuerit,* 1 mart. 1929, art. 32—*AAS,* XXI (1929), 158; Bouscaren, *The Canon Law Digest,* I, 14.

## CHAPTER V

## THE RECEPTION OF HOLY COMMUNION

### Article I. Devotional Communion

The law of canon 866, § 1, which allows the faithful to receive Holy Communion in any Rite, even for the sake of devotion, is a law that is not of traditional character. The faithful of the Latin Rite were long forbidden to receive Holy Communion in leavened bread from a priest of an Oriental Rite, unless an apostolic indult allowed them to do so.[1] On the other hand, Catholics belonging to Oriental Rites, who usually receive Holy Communion in leavened bread, were allowed to receive the Holy Eucharist in unleavened bread from a Latin priest in a Latin Church, if there was no church or no priest of their own Rite in the place. However, if together with a Latin Church there existed a church of their own Rite in the place, then the faithful of the Oriental Church had to communicate according to their own proper Rite.[2]

The precept that everyone was to receive Holy Communion in his own Rite was a general rule repeated many times by the Holy See. It was only in the case of necessity that the faithful were permitted to receive the Eucharist consecrated in another Rite, when between their own Rite and some other Rite there existed a difference in the use of leavened or unleavened bread.[3] By law there were granted only two exceptions which permitted a person to receive

[1] Benedictus XIV, const. *Etsi pastoralis*, 26 maii 1742, § VI, n. XII—*Fontes*, n. 328; *Collect.*, n. 338. S. C. de Prop. Fide, instr. 30 apr. 1862, n. 3—*Fontes*, n. 4857; *Collect.*, n. 1228. Decr. 6 oct. 1863—*Fontes*, n. 4859; *Collect.*, n. 1243.

[2] Const. *Etsi pastoralis, ibid.*, nn. XIII, XIV—*Fontes*, n. 328; S. C. de Prop. Fide, decr. 18 aug. 1893—*Fontes*, n. 4926; *Collect.*, n. 1846; litt. encycl. 26 febr. 1896—*Fontes*, n. 4934; *Collect.*, n. 1919.

[3] S. C. S. Off., 4 sept. 1721—*Collect.*, n. 296; decr. 12 dec. 1821—*Fontes*, n. 864; S. C. de Prop. Fide, 11 dec. 1838, nn. 12, 23—*Fontes*, n. 4778; *Collect.*, n. 879; instr. 30 apr. 1862, n. 2—*Fontes*, n. 4857; *Collect.*, n. 1228; decr. 6 oct. 1863, C, b—*Fontes*, n. 4859; *Collect.*, n. 1243.

Holy Communion in a Rite not his own: (1) if a priest of the recipient's own Rite could not be had, then a person could receive Holy Viaticum in another Rite from a priest of that Rite, and (2) if a priest of the recipient's own Rite could not be had, then a person could fulfill the Paschal precept by receiving Holy Communion in another Rite from a priest of that Rite. This was apparent in the language of repeatedly issued documents among which the following are worthy of special mention.[4]

Oriental Catholics could receive the Holy Eucharist in unleavened bread from a Latin priest when they were not able to receive Holy Communion in their own Rite from a priest of their own Rite. The Sacred Congregation for the Propagation of the Faith gave two rules that had to be observed by the Catholics of an Oriental Rite who usually communicated in leavened bread: (1) they could not receive in unleavened bread as long as it was possible for them to receive in their own Rite in leavened bread; (2) when there was difficulty for receiving in leavened bread, they could receive in unleavened bread in order to fulfill the Paschal precept and in order to receive Holy Viaticum, and also in the cases mentioned by Pope Benedict XIV in his Instruction *"Eo quamvis tempore,"* § *Neque etiam.*[5] This instruction of Pope Benedict XIV provided for the Latin missionaries laboring in Egypt to help the Coptic priests in administering to the faithful of the Coptic Rite just as they administer to their own Latin Catholics.

The Holy Office, however, granted to the Patriarch of Cilicia

[4] S. C. de Prop. Fide, decr. 6 oct. 1863, C, d—*Fontes*, n. 4859; *Collect.*, n. 1243; instr. 30 apr. 1862—*loc. cit.*; S. C. de Prop. Fide pro negotiis ritus orientalis, 25 ian. 1864—*Coll. Lac.*, II, 564, b (art. C, § d).

[5] S. C. de Prop. Fide, instr. (ad Deleg. Ap. Aegypti), 30 apr. 1862, n. 2: "Due regole sonosi stabilite per gli utenti del fermentato: la 1°. è che non possono ad arbitrio communicarsi in azimo quando abbiano la opportunità di farlo nel proprio rito; la 2°. è che quando si verifichi la difficoltà di communicarsi in fermentato, lo possono fare anche in azimo non solo in articolo di morte e per adempire al precetto pasquale, ma anche in altri casi come si stabilisce nella instruzione pastorale di Benedetto XIV, *Eo quamvis tempore*, § *Neque etiam.*"—*Fontes*, n. 4857. Cf. Benedictus XIV, instr. *Eo quamvis tempore*, 4 maii 1745, § 16—*Fontes*, n. 357; cf. also S. C. de Prop. Fide, litt. 11 oct. 1780—*Fontes*, n. 4584; S. C. de Prop. Fide (C. G.), 25 iul. 1887, § 6, b—*Fontes*, n. 4920.

the faculty of dispensing Armenian Catholics living in the town of Diyarbékir, so that, while they lacked priests of their own Rite, they could communicate in leavened bread from a priest of the Chaldean Rite, in order that they might thus fulfill the Paschal precept or be enabled to receive Holy Viaticum.[6] This faculty was extended by the Sacred Congregation for the Propagation of the Faith to all Catholics who communicated in unleavened bread. These Catholics, if they found themselves among Catholics who usually communicated in leavened bread, could communicate in leavened bread in order to fulfill the Paschal precept or be enabled to receive Holy Viaticum.[7]

Catholics of an Oriental Rite, who usually communicated in unleavened bread (the Armenians, the Maronites, the Chaldeans in Malabar, the Syro-Malabars and the Italo-Greeks in a few churches in Sicily, in southern Italy and in places belonging to the monastery of the Mother of God at Grottaferrata), could receive Holy Communion from a priest who also consecrated the Holy Eucharist in unleavened bread, namely, a Latin priest, an Armenian priest, or a Maronite priest, or a priest of one of the other Rites mentioned. But a pontifical dispensation was necessary if they were lawfully to receive Holy Communion consecrated in leavened bread.[8]

Catholics of an Oriental Rite who usually communicated in leavened bread were given permission to receive Holy Communion in a Latin Church, provided that they received in leavened bread and from a priest of their own Rite.[9]

On July 25, 1887, the Sacred Congregation for the Propagation of the Faith answered several questions proposed to it regarding the reception of Holy Communion in a Rite different from the one to which the recipient belonged. One of the questions asked was whether a Catholic who belonged to an Oriental Rite which con-

[6] 12 dec. 1821—*Fontes,* n. 864; *Fonti,* I, *Testi Vari di Diritto Nuovo,* 199; *Collect.,* n. 879, ad 23, in nota.

[7] 11 dec. 1838 (C. G.), n. 23: " . . . quoad vero communicantes in azymo, concedantur facultates prout in decreto S. O. 12 dec. 1821."—*Fontes,* n. 4778.

[8] S. C. de Prop. Fide, instr. 30 apr. 1862, n. 3—*Fontes,* n. 4857.

[9] S. C. de Prop. Fide, instr. (ad Deleg. Ap. Aegypti), 30 apr. 1862, n. 2—*Fontes,* n. 4857; *Collect.,* n. 1228.

secrated the Holy Eucharist in leavened bread could receive Holy Communion in unleavened bread from a Latin priest when there was no priest of his own Rite in the place, although there was a priest of another Oriental Rite who consecrated the Holy Eucharist in leavened bread. The answer of the Sacred Congregation was that even though the various Instructions permitted an Oriental Catholic to receive Holy Communion in the Latin Rite from a Latin priest when there was no priest of his own Rite present, nevertheless, in this case, the Oriental Catholic should receive Holy Communion from the priest of the other Oriental Rite who consecrated in leavened bread.[10]

The Sacred Congregation for the Propagation of the Faith in a decree on August 18, 1893, adverted to the fact that a large number of the faithful of different Rites were intermingled in some regions, many of them not having a church or a priest of their own Rite. For that reason, as well as for the sake of encouraging their devotion, the Sacred Congregation gave permission for the faithful to receive Holy Communion according to the Rite of the church existing in the place, provided it was a Catholic Church, even outside of the two cases in which such a reception had previously been made permissible by the law, namely, in order to receive Holy Viaticum and to fulfill the Paschal precept.[11]

Pope Leo XIII (1878-1903) in his Apostolic Letter, *Orientalium,* extended this permission of the Sacred Congregation for the Propagation of the Faith to have its full operative effect even in the case when the church of one's own Rite was so far away that one could go there only with great inconvenience. However, the ordinary was

[10] 25 iul. 1887, n. 6, a—*Fontes,* n. 4920; *Collect.,* n. 1679.

[11] Decr. 18 aug. 1893: This decree was the result of a special audience which Pope Leo XIII had on July 2, 1893, with the Fathers of the Sacred Congregation for the Propagation of the Faith in which the Holy Father ordered that a decree be published and promulgated granting this privilege: " . . . omnibus fidelibus cuiuscumque ritus, sive latini, sive orientalis, degentibus in locis, in quibus non sit ecclesia aut sacerdos proprii ritus, facultas in posterum a S. Sede conceditur Sanctissimam Communionem, non modo in articulo mortis et pro paschali praecepto adimplendo, sed etiam *quovis tempore devotionis gratia,* iuxta ritum ecclesiae existentis in praedictis locis, dummodo catholica sit, recipiendi."—*Fontes,* n. 4926; *Collect.,* n. 1846.

to be the judge of such circumstances.[12] In the same letter, the Pope also regulated the question of the parochial status and rights in relation to Orientals who had no priest or church of their own Rite, in accordance with which Holy Viaticum and Paschal Communion were to be received at the hands of their pastor. Since these Oriental Catholics had no pastor of their own Rite, the pastor of another Rite in whose territory they lived was to take spiritual care of them and administer to them.[13]

The Apostolic Letter, *Orientalium,* of Pope Leo XIII changed the ruling of the 1893 decree since the Orientals now had their own proper pastor, even though he might belong to a different Rite. The Sacred Congregation for the Propagation of the Faith adverted to this change, and in an encyclical letter indicated that accordingly the decree of 1893 applied for the future only to the case of devotional Communion. Holy Viaticum and the Paschal Communion were to be received from their own proper pastor according to the rule made by Pope Leo XIII in the Apostolic Letter, *Orientalium.* The encyclical letter of 1896 also stated that Catholic Orientals, who communicate in leavened bread and who are in a place where there are only Latin priests or priests of an Oriental Rite who consecrate in unleavened bread, should place themselves under the jurisdiction of the Oriental priest of their choice as long as they remain in that place.[14]

The Constitution, *Tradita ab antiquis,* of Pope Pius X allowed every Catholic to receive the Holy Eucharist in any Catholic Rite, even for the sake of devotion.[15] This provision was incorporated some few years later in the present Code of Canon Law of the Latin Church in canon 866, § 1:

> "Omnibus fidelibus cuiusvis ritus datur facultas ut, *pietatis causa,* sacramentum Eucharisticum quolibet ritu confectum suscipiunt."

[12] Litt. ap. *Orientalium,* 30 nov. 1894, II—*Fontes,* n. 627.

[13] Litt. ap. *Orientalium, loc. cit.*—*Fontes,* n. 627.

[14] S. C. de Prop. Fide, litt. encycl. 26 febr. 1896—*Fontes,* n. 4934; *Collect.,* n. 1919.

[15] 14 sept. 1912, n. III—*Fontes,* n. 698.

This canon includes in its scope Oriental Catholics as well as Latin Catholics. The law of Pope Pius X and of canon 866, § 1, was repeated in the decree of the Sacred Oriental Congregation on March 1, 1929, for the Greek-Ruthenians in the United States.[16]

Both canon 866, § 1, and the decree *Cum data fuerit* make it clear that the restrictions placed on the faithful to receive Holy Communion in another Rite, which were strict in the past, do not bind now. The words "*pietatis causa*" in the canon and in the decree, signify that no particular reason at all is necessary for a person to receive Holy Communion in a Rite not his own. Cappello explains how the words "*pietatis causa*" are to be understood:

> "Verba *pietatis causa* ita sunt intelligenda ut unicuique liceat sacram communionem recipere in azymo vel fermentato non solum quando urget necessitas seu causa gravis, sed etiam sola devotionis gratia, i. e. *absque ulla peculiari ratione*." [17]

This was also the mind of Pope Leo XIII when in an audience he approved a declaration of the Pontifical Commission for the reunion of the Churches. The declaration permitted a person, *for devotional causes,* to receive Holy Communion in leavened bread on one day, and in unleavened bread on the next day.[18]

The faithful are at liberty, then, to receive Holy Communion in any Catholic Rite, even under both species, whenever out of devotion they so desire. The Catholics of the Latin Rite may receive Holy Communion in a church of an Oriental Rite; Catholics of Oriental Rites may receive Holy Communion in a church of the Latin Rite, or in the church of another Oriental Rite.[19]

[16] S. C. Or., decr. *Cum data fuerit,* 1 mart. 1929, art. 32—*AAS,* XXI (1929), 158. Bouscaren, *The Canon Law Digest,* I, 14.

[17] *De Sacramentis,* I, n. 494. In his first edition, which appeared in 1921, Cappello indicated that if there were some *incommodum* preventing the reception of Holy Communion according to one's own Rite, then a person could receive according to another Rite.—I, n. 524.

[18] 14 febr. 1896 as cited in Gasparri, *De Eucharistia,* II, n. 1178.

[19] Noldin, *Theologia Moralis,* III, n. 107, § 1, c.: " . . . quivis catholicus communionem sumere potest ad libitum in quavis ecclesia catholica cuiuslibet ritus." Cf. Woywod, *A Practical Commentary on the Code of Canon Law,* I, n. 765.

## Article II. Easter Communion

The law in the past always insisted that the faithful receive Holy Communion in their own Rite in order to fulfill the Paschal precept. It was only by way of exception to this law that the faithful were permitted to fulfill the Paschal precept by receiving Holy Communion in another Rite. The faithful could receive the Easter Communion in another Rite only when it was impossible for them to receive in their own Rite, either because there was no church of their own Rite or no priest of their own Rite in the place where they were living.[20]

It must be remembered that this permission was granted for exceptional cases only. The law still demanded that everyone should receive Easter Communion in his own Rite. The letters of the Popes, as well as the instructions and decrees of the Sacred Congregations, continued to insist that each one fulfill the Paschal precept by receiving Holy Communion in his own Rite and from his own pastor.[21] The law which insisted that every one should receive the Easter Communion in his own Rite was also implied in other decrees, which allowed the faithful to receive Holy Communion in another Rite in order that they might fulfill the Paschal precept when it was impossible for them to receive in their own Rite from a priest of their own Rite.[22]

[20] S. C. S. Off., decr. 12 dec. 1821—*Fontes*, n. 864; *Fonti*, I, 199; S. C. de Prop. Fide (C. G.), 11 dec. 1838, n. 23—*Fontes*, n. 4778; *Collect.*, n. 879; (C. G.), 25 iul. 1887, ad 6, b—*Fontes*, n. 4920; *Collect.*, n. 1679; decr. 18 aug. 1893—*Fontes*, n. 4926; *Collect.*, n. 1846.

[21] Benedictus XIV, const. *Etsi pastoralis*, 26 maii 1742, § VI, n. XII—*Fontes*, n. 328. Pius X (const. *Tradita ab antiquis*, 14 sept. 1912, n. IV): "Quisque fidelium praecepto Communionis paschalis ita satisfaciet, si eam suo ritu accipiat et quidem a parocho suo: cui sane in ceteris obeundis religionis officiis addictus manebit."—*Fontes*, n. 698. Cf. S. C. de Prop. Fide, instr. (ad Deleg. Ap. Aegypti), n. 2—*Fontes*, n. 4857; *Collect.*, n. 1228; litt. encycl. 26 febr. 1896—*Fontes*, n. 4934; *Collect.*, n. 1919. Cf. also S. C. S. Off. decr. 4 sept. 1721—*Collect.*, n. 296.

[22] Const. *Etsi pastoralis*, *ibid.*, n. XIII—*Fontes*, n. 328; S. C. S. Off., 12 dec. 1821—*Fontes*, n. 864; S. C. de Prop. Fide (C. G.), 11 dec. 1838—*Fontes*, n. 4778; *Collect.*, n. 879; decr. 6 oct. 1863, C, b—*Fontes*, n. 4859; *Collect.*, n. 1243; (C. G.), 25 iul. 1887, ad 6, b—*Fontes*, n. 4920; decr. 18 aug. 1893—*Fontes*, n. 4926.

The gradual relaxation of the law to receive Holy Communion in one's own Rite was not extended to the Easter Communion. The faithful were still bound to receive the Easter Communion in their own Rite from their pastor or from a priest of their own Rite. The permission granted in the decrees of the Roman Congregations to the faithful for allowing them to fulfill the Paschal precept by receiving Holy Communion in another Rite, was still only for cases of necessity. The Sacred Congregation for the Propagation of the Faith in a decree for the Oriental Church legislated that the faithful fulfill their Easter duty only if they receive Holy Communion in their own Rite and from their own pastor.[23]

Even the Apostolic Letter *Orientalium* of Pope Leo XIII and the Constitution *Tradita ab antiquis* of Pope Pius X, both of which granted so much freedom to the faithful by permitting them to receive Holy Communion in another Rite for the sake of devotion, excepted Easter Communion and still demanded that each one receive Easter Communion in his own Rite (excluding a case of necessity, when it was licit to fulfill the Paschal precept by receiving Holy Communion in another Rite).[24]

The Code of Canon Law of the Latin Church, in canon 866, § 2, was more liberal than the earlier decrees of the Popes and of the Congregations. Rather than impose a precept so as to command everyone to receive Easter Communion in his own Rite, as the former legislation had done, canon 866, § 2, counsels each one to receive Easter Communion in his own Rite.

> "Suadendum tamen ut suo quisque ritu fideles praecepto communionis paschalis satisfaciant."

Although the Code in canon 866, §2, permits more freedom than the law in the past had done, nevertheless the law to satisfy the Paschal precept in one's own Rite does not extend as much liberty

[23] S. C. de Prop. Fide pro negotiis Ritus Orientalis, decr. *Cum Episcopo,* 18 aug. 1914, art. 24: "Quisque fidelium praecepto Communionis paschalis ita satisfaciet, si eam suo ritu et quidem a parocho suo accipiat."—*AAS,* VI (1914), 462.

[24] Litt. ap. *Orientalium,* 30 nov. 1894, § II—*Fontes,* n. 627; const. *Tradita ab antiquis,* 14 sept. 1912, n. IV—*Fontes,* n. 698. Cf. also S. C. de Prop. Fide, decr. 18 aug. 1893—*Fontes,* n. 4926; *Collect.,* n. 1846.

to receive Holy Communion in another Rite as does canon 866, § 1, for the reception of devotional Communion. According to canon 866, § 1, the faithful are allowed to receive Holy Communion, for the sake of devotion, in any Rite they wish and whenever they wish. But canon 866, § 2, shows that the Church desires the faithful to receive Easter Communion in their own Rite, if they have the opportunity. Moreover, canon 859, § 3, also shows that the law desires that the faithful receive Easter Communion not only in their own Rite, but also in their own parish church.

> "Suadendum fidelibus ut huic praecepto satisfaciant in sua quisque paroecia; et qui in aliena paroecia satisfecerint, curent proprium parochum de adimpleto praecepto certiorem facere."

From the terminology of canon 866, § 2, and canon 859, § 3, the law to receive Easter Communion in their own Rite, it is apparent, cannot be taken as a precept, but rather as a counsel. According to Cicognani, *suadendum* cannot be understood in the sense of *praescribendum,* but rather has the meaning of *consilium dandum.*[25] Cappello also holds that this law to receive Easter Communion in their own Rite is not a precept, but simply a counsel which does not bind even *sub levi.*[26]

Canon 859, § 3, and canon 866, § 2, oblige pastors and others who have the care of souls to advise the faithful that each one should satisfy his Easter duty by receiving Holy Communion in his own Rite and in his own parish church. Those who receive Easter Communion in another church should inform their pastor of the fulfillment of their Easter duty. The Synod of Mount Lebanon made the same law for the Maronites in 1736. This Synod legislated that the pastor must have a list of his parishioners and must see to it that they communicate during the Paschal time. If some of his

[25] Cicognani (*Commentarium ad Librum I Codicis* [Romae: Ex Schola Typographica "Pio X," 1925]), p. 338: "Nullo modo potest illud *suadendum*—quod novum non est et in aliis canonibus recurrit—trahi ad sensum verbi *praescribere*: *suadere* idem est ac *consilium dare, consiliis et hortamentis inducere, minime praecepto obstringere.*"

[26] *De Sacramentis,* I, par. 494: "Merum consilium est, et non praeceptum, adeo ut ne *sub levi* quidem obliget."

parishoners were unmindful of the warning to receive during the Easter time, the pastor must report them to the ordinary. If the faithful have received in another parish, they must notify their pastor of this fact.[27]

The decree *Cum Episcopo* of the Sacred Congregation for the Propagation of the Faith, issued in 1914 for the Greek-Ruthenians in the United States, also demanded that the faithful satisfy the Paschal precept by receiving Holy Communion in their own Rite and from their own pastor.[28]

The obligation enacted in canons 859, § 3, and 866, § 2, is imposed on the pastors or on those who have the care of souls. It is they who are to advise the faithful to receive Easter Communion in their own parish church and in their own Rite. The faithful should receive their Easter Communion in their own parish church and in their own Rite, if it is possible for them to do so. However, even if the faithful receive Easter Communion in another parish or in another Rite, whether inadvertently or even deliberately, they satisfy the Paschal precept. In the event that one of the faithful receives Easter Communion in another parish or in another Rite, he shall inform his pastor of this.

Considering canon 1, in virtue of which the law of the Code does not include Orientals, the Apostolic Delegate of Egypt asked the Holy See whether canon 866, § 2, abrogated for the Orientals the Constitution *Tradita ab antiquis* of Pope Pius X, which stated that all the faithful must receive Holy Communion in their own Rite in order to fulfill the Paschal precept. The Sacred Oriental Congregation replied in the negative, namely, that canon 866, § 2, did not abrogate the Constitution *Tradita ab antiquis* for the Orientals, and that they are still bound by its prescriptions to receive Easter Communion in their own Rite.[29]

A later response of the same Congregation stated that the faith-

[27] Synodus Montis Libani (1736), pars II, cap. XII, § 18—*Coll. Lac.*, II, 205.

[28] Decr. 18 aug. 1914, art. 24—*AAS*, VI (1914), 462.

[29] S. C. Or., 31 oct. 1922: " . . . La Cost. Ap. *Tradita ab antiquis* è tuttora in vigora, non essendo mai stata revocata." Cicognani (*Commentarium ad Librum I Codicis*, p. 14) adds: "Quae verba finalia exclusive se referunt ad Orientales."

ful of the Oriental Rites commit a mortal sin and do not satisfy the Paschal precept if they receive Easter Communion solely in the Latin Rite. This response must be understood as applying to the faithful of the Oriental Rite who are in their own territory where it is possible for them to receive Easter Communion in their own Rite. The response does not apply to those who are living among Catholics of the Latin Rite and have no church of their own Rite where they can fulfill their Easter duty.[30]

This interpretation was changed entirely by subsequent decrees of the Sacred Oriental Congregation. On January 26, 1925, the Sacred Congregation discussed some doubts about the interpretation of canon 866, and declared that both the Orientals and Latins satisfy the precept of receiving Holy Communion during Easter time if they communicate in another Rite.[31]

The decree *Cum data fuerit,* issued in 1929 for the Ruthenians in the United States, also abrogated the previous legislation of the decree *Cum Episcopo,* which required Catholics of the Oriental Rite, as not included in the prescription of canon 866, § 2, to satisfy their Easter duty by receiving Holy Communion in their own Rite. This decree allows anyone, no matter to what Oriental Rite he belongs, validly and licitly to fulfill the Paschal precept, even if he receives Easter Communion in another Rite. However, the decree repeats canon 866, § 2, and canon 859, § 3, that the faithful should be persuaded to receive Easter Communion in their own Rite and in their own parish; if they fulfill their Easter duty in another parish or in another Rite, they should inform their own pastor of this.[32]

Canon 859, § 3, and canon 866, § 2, then, include in effect Catholics of the Latin Rite and of the Oriental Rites in their provisions. Anyone of the faithful, therefore, can obviously fulfill his Easter duty by receiving Holy Communion in his own parish church and in his own Rite. He can also, however, fulfill his Easter duty,

[30] S. C. Or., 14 apr. 1924—Cicognani, *ibid.,* p. 15.

[31] S. C. Or., decr. 26 ian. 1925: " . . . tum orientales, tum latinos praecepto communionis paschalis satisfacere, si alieno ritu communicent."—Cicognani, *ibid.,* p. 339.

[32] S. C. Or., decr. *Cum data fuerit,* 1 mart. 1929, art. 33—*AAS,* XXI (1929), 158. Bouscaren, *The Canon Law Digest,* I, 14.

validly and licitly, by receiving Holy Communion in another parish church or in another Rite, whether he does so inadvertently or purposely. When the faithful have fulfilled their Easter duty outside their parish or in another Rite they must inform the pastor about it. The pastor, on the other hand, should try to persuade the faithful to receive Easter Communion in their own parish church and in their own Rite. If the faithful do not follow the pastor's advice, they do not act illicitly by receiving Easter Communion in another parish or in another Rite, and the pastor whom they approach can and must administer Holy Communion to the faithful, even to one who he knows belongs to another Rite. The pastor himself does not act illicitly in administering Holy Communion, even Easter Communion, to a person who belongs to another Rite.

## Article III. Holy Viaticum

According to the almost unanimous teaching of theologians, the divine law commands each one of the faithful to receive Holy Viaticum when in danger of death.[83] The ecclesiastical law has always insisted that the faithful receive Holy Viaticum in their own Rite. The Code made no change in the former legislation, which commanded the faithful to receive Holy Viaticum in their own Rite, as it has in the legislation for devotional Communion and the Easter Communion. The only exception made by the Code in the law requiring the receiving of the Viaticum in one's own Rite is the exception which was made also in the laws of the past. Both the former legislation and the Code permit the faithful licitly to receive Holy Viaticum, in the case of urgent necessity, in any Rite. Canon 866, § 3, states this law and the exception:

> "Sanctum Viaticum moribundis ritu proprio accipiendum est; sed, *urgente necessitate,* fas esto quolibet ritu illud accipere."

In paragraph 3, canon 866 does not permit the freedom which it

[83] Cappello, *De Sacramentis,* I, n. 421, § 2. Davis, *Moral and Pastoral Theology,* III, 227. Prümmer, *Theologia Moralis,* III, § 208, n. 2. Merkelbach, *Summa Theologiae Moralis,* III, § 294, b. Noldin, *Theologia Moralis,* III, § 137, n. 1. Lehmkuhl, *Theologia Moralis,* II, § 195. Tanquerey, *Synopsis Theologiae Dogmaticae,* III, § 918.

grants in paragraphs 1 and 2. Canon 866, § 1, permits the faithful to receive Holy Communion in another Rite, for the sake of devotion, without any special reason and whenever they so desire. Paragraph 2 counsels each one to satisfy the Paschal precept by receiving Holy Communion in his own Rite. But if a person receives his Easter Communion in another Rite, inadvertently or even deliberately, he nevertheless fulfills the Paschal precept and is not guilty of any sin, mortal or venial. Canon 866, § 3, on the other hand, is truly a precept and imposes an obligation on the faithful to receive Holy Viaticum in their own Rite.

The same obligation to receive Holy Viaticum in one's own Rite was also imposed on the faithful by the former decrees of the Holy See; however, the exception by which it was lawful to receive Holy Viaticum in another Rite in the case of necessity was always granted. The case of necessity implied in the decrees of the Sacred Congregations as in canon 866, § 3, could arise: (1) when there was no priest of the prospective recipient's own Rite present to administer Holy Viaticum to the dying person in his own Rite, and (2) when a priest of the dying person's own Rite was present, but when at the same time there was not available for him any sacred host consecrated in his own Rite. The Letter of the Sacred Congregation for the Propagation of the Faith made this clear when it forbade Latin missionaries to administer the Sacraments to Catholics of the Oriental Rite when there was a priest of their own Rite present. But the missionaries of the Latin Rite were authorized to administer the Sacrament of Holy Viaticum in the case of necessity to dying Catholics of an Oriental Rite and in species consecrated according to the Latin Rite.[84]

The Holy Office granted to the Patriarch of Cilicia the faculty of dispensing Armenian Catholics (who usually communicate in unleavened bread) living in the town of Diyarbékir, in order that, the while they lacked priests of their own Rite, they might communicate in leavened bread at the hands of a priest of the Chaldean Rite, and thus not be deprived of Holy Viaticum.[85] A like privilege was

[84] Litt. 11 oct. 1780—*Fontes,* n. 4584.

[85] 12 dec. 1821—*Fontes,* n. 864; *Fonti,* I, 199; *Collect.,* n. 879, ad 23am, in nota.

granted by the Sacred Congregation for the Propagation of the Faith in an Instruction for the Greek-Ruthenian and Latin Bishops in the province of Lemberg.[36]

Pope Pius X, in his Constitution *Tradita ab antiquis,* set down the law for the reception of Holy Viaticum:

> "Sanctum Viaticum moribundis ritu proprio de manibus proprii parochi accipiendum est: sed, urgente necessitate, fas esto a sacerdote quolibet illud accipere; qui tamen ritu suo ministrabit."[37]

This law was incorporated, almost word for word, in the Code of Canon Law in canon 866, § 3.

Oriental Catholics of the Ruthenian Rite in the United States received the same legislation in the decrees *Cum Episcopo* and *Cum data fuerit.* Both decrees in their law for the reception of Holy Viaticum used the exact words employed by Pope Pius X in his constitution *Tradita ab antiquis.*[38]

Since it appears to be a command of the divine law that the faithful receive Holy Viaticum when they are in danger of death, it was necessary that the law of the Church make an exception to her own positive law which prescribes that the faithful receive Holy Viaticum in their own Rite. And this the Church has always done in legislating for the reception of Holy Viaticum. In order that the faithful may fulfill the divine precept of receiving the Holy Eucharist when they are in danger of death, the ecclesiastical law permits the faithful to receive Holy Viaticum in any Catholic Rite when it is impossible for them to receive in their own Rite.

[36] Sacrum vero viaticum etiam infirmis nonnisi juxta eorum ritum a propriis ritus sacerdote porrigi debet. Deficiente autem sacerdote proprii ritus valeat ex Apostolico indulto Latinus a presbytero Rutheno in fermentato, et Ruthenus infirmus a presbytero Latino in azymo sacrum viaticum accipere."—S. C. de Prop. Fide pro negotiis ritus orientalis, decr. 6 oct. 1863—*Coll. Lac.,* II, 564 b (art. C, d); *Fontes,* n. 4859; *Collect.,* n. 1243.

[37] 14 sept. 1912, n. V—*Fontes,* n. 698.

[38] S. C. de Prop. Fide pro negotiis ritus orientalis, decr. *Cum Episcopo,* 18 aug. 1914, art. 25—*AAS,* VI (1914), 462; S. C. Or., decr. *Cum data fuerit,* 1 mart. 1929, art. 34—*AAS,* XXI (1929), 158. Bouscaren, *The Canon Law Digest,* I, 14.

## Article IV. Infant Communion

For a long time the custom of communicating infants existed both in the Western and in the Eastern Church. The IV General Council of the Lateran (1215) and the Council of Trent (1545-1563) declared that children who had not as yet attained the use of reason were not obliged by any necessity to receive Holy Communion, and anyone was condemned who said that they were. This custom gradually fell into disuse also among the Oriental Rites, and they recognized the fact that to administer Holy Communion to infants was unnecessary. But wherever this ancient custom was still in practice, the Holy See did not condemn it.

The custom of administering Holy Communion to infants had gradually lost its popularity among the Oriental Rites. Since the IV General Council of Lateran (1215) and the Council of Trent (1545-1563) had legislated for the Western Church that only those who had attained the use of reason were obliged to receive Holy Communion, practically all the Catholic Oriental Rites have also discontinued the ancient custom of administering Holy Communion to infants. Among the Oriental Rites which no longer prescribe the administration of the Holy Eucharist to infants are the Maronites, the Syrians, the Italo-Greeks, the Armenians and the Copts. The Melkites and the Ruthenians permitted the practice of administering Holy Communion to infants only where this custom was in force and could not be easily discontinued, although they recognized that there was no necessity which obliged infants to receive Holy Communion.

The Sacred Congregation for the Propagation of the Faith, when asked by the Melkites whether it was expedient to administer the Holy Eucharist to infants immediately after they were baptized, replied that infants were not obliged by any necessity to receive Holy Communion; but where this ancient custom was in force, it was not to be condemned.[39]

Pope Benedict XIV forbade the Italo-Greeks to administer Holy Communion to infants, but he recognized the fact that this practice

[39] Resp. 5 apr. 1729—*Coll. Lac.*, II, n. 442; *Fonti*, XV, *Droit Particulier des Melkites* (1724-1923), n. 116; Mansi, XLVI, 94.

was customary among the Greeks.[40] And the Synod of Mount Lebanon (1736) prescribed for the Maronites that the Holy Eucharist should in no manner be given to children and infants until they had attained the use of reason in accordance with the teaching of the Council of Trent.[41]

The practice of giving Holy Communion to newly baptized infants was prescribed for the Copts by the Sacred Congregation of the Holy Office, but the necessary precautions were to be observed.[42] Later on the *Synodus Alexandrina Coptorum,* held in Cairo, Egypt, on January 18, 1898, while admitting that infants and children who did not as yet have the use of reason were capable of receiving Holy Communion, nevertheless stated that infants and children who lacked the use of reason were not obliged by any necessity to receive the Holy Eucharist. The Synod then continued by declaring that the discipline in force in the Coptic Church at that time was to be preserved whereby the administration of Holy Communion was to be deferred until the children understood the excellence of this Sacrament and could receive the Holy Eucharist for the first time with the required dispositions.[43]

The Synod of Zamość (1720) in legislating for the Ruthenians recognized that the practice of administering the Holy Eucharist to infants and to children who had not yet reached the use of reason was a very old custom; however, the Synod ordered that this custom should be discontinued if this could be done without scandal.[44]

The Syrians had permitted the administration of Holy Communion to infants after their baptism. The priest let a few drops of the Precious Blood fall into the child's mouth immediately after the child

[40] Const. *Etsi pastoralis,* 26 maii 1742, § II, n. VII—*Fontes,* n. 328.

[41] Pars II, cap. XII, n. 13—*Coll. Lac.,* 200-201; *Fonti,* XII, *Ius Particulare Maronitarum,* n. 316.

[42] Decr. 14 iun. 1741—*Collect.,* n. 713.

[43] *Synodus Alexandrina Coptorum habiti* [*a?*] *Cairi in Aegypto anno 1898* (Romae: Typis Polyglottis S. C. de Prop. Fide, 1899), sect. II, cap. 3, art. IV, pars I, n. VI, §§ I and II.

[44] Synod of Zamošć (1720), tit. III, § 1-a—*Fonti,* XI, n. 236. Cf. also tit. III, § 3-a—*Fonti,* XI, n. 235.

was baptized.[45] This practice was later changed by the National Synod of the Syrians held on Mount Lebanon on July 22, 1888. This Synod prescribed the administration of the Holy Eucharist was to be delayed until the children understood the importance of this excellent and august Sacrament, and until they could approach the altar to receive Holy Communion with the necessary dispositions.[46]

The custom of administering Holy Communion to infants is, however, still in force among the Greeks.[47]

[45] *Fonti,* Series II, XXVII, *Disciplina Antiochena Antica—Siri,* nn. 54-56, 160.

[46] *Synodus Sciarfensis Syrorum in Monte Libano Celebrata,* 22 iul. 1888 (Romae: Typis Polyglottis S. C. de Prop. Fide, 1896), cap. V, art. IV, § 5, n. III.

[47] Benedict XIV, const. *Etsi pastoralis,* § II, n. VII—*Fontes,* n. 328; Cappello, *De Sacramentis,* I, n. 799, § 2.

# CONCLUSIONS

1. A priest validly consecrates the Holy Eucharist in either leavened or unleavened bread. He licitly consecrates bread in the form proper to another Rite only when he must complete the sacrifice, that is when after he has consecrated the chalice he discovers that the bread is invalid matter, and the only other bread available in that which exists in a form that is proper to another Rite; or when, contrary to the opinion of some authors, it is necessary for the priest to administer the Holy Viaticum, and he has no bread which in its form is proper to his own Rite; or when the priest has an apostolic indult to consecrate the Holy Eucharist in a form of bread that is proper to another Rite.

2. A priest may celebrate Mass in a church of another Rite, even though there are churches of his own Rite available, provided that he uses an altar of his own Rite and has obtained permission from the rector of the church in which he wishes to celebrate. A priest can use the Greek *Antimension* only if he has an apostolic indult to do so, but he must follow the prescriptions stated in the indult for its use.

3. Priests of Oriental Rites who have their own proper Oriental ordinary in this country must receive their celebret from him. Other Oriental priests who are subject to the jurisdiction of Latin ordinaries must obtain their celebret from the Latin ordinary in whose diocese they have established their domicile according to the rules laid down by the Sacred Oriental Congregation. A priest of an Oriental Rite who is in this country for some purpose other than that of administering to the faithful of his own Rite and is subject to no ordinary in the United States must have with him his celebret and his credentials obtained from the Sacred Oriental Congregation. A priest of an Oriental Rite coming to this country even to administer to the faithful of his own Rite must present the celebret of the Sacred Oriental Congregation to the local ordinary in whose diocese he is to labor.

4. Even when there is no case of necessity urging it, a priest may administer Holy Communion which was consecrated in another Rite

provided that the form of bread used for confecting the Sacrament is the same as the form of bread used by the priest in his own Rite. In order that a priest may distribute Holy Communion in a form of bread that is proper to another Rite, the case of necessity need not be so urgent as the danger of death, but it must be more serious than merely for the purpose of administering Holy Communion to the faithful who want to receive the Holy Eucharist out of devotion.

5. The faithful are at liberty to receive Holy Communion in any Catholic Rite, even under both species, whenever out of devotion they so desire. No further reasons at all are necessary. The pastor, Latin and Oriental, should persuade the faithful to receive Easter Communion in their own Rite and in their own parish church, but the faithful licitly fulfill the Paschal precept even though they receive Easter Communion in another Rite and in another church. A person can receive the Holy Viaticum which was consecrated in a form of bread that is proper to another Rite only when there is no priest of his own Rite present, or when a priest of his own Rite is indeed present but has at his avail only the Holy Eucharist which was consecrated in a form of bread that is proper to another Rite.

# BIBLIOGRAPHY

## Sources

*Acta Apostolicae Sedis, Commentarium Officiale,* Romae, 1909—

*Acta et Decreta Sacrorum Conciliorum Recentiorum, Collectio Lacensis,* 7 vols., Friburgi Brisgoviae, 1870-1890.

Berger, Élie, *Les Registres D'Innocent IV,* 4 vols., Parisiis, 1884-1897.

Bouscaren, T. Lincoln, *The Canon Law Digest,* 2 vols., Milwaukee: The Bruce Publishing Company, Vol. I, 1934, and Vol. II, 1943.

*Codex Iuris Canonici Pii X Pontificis Maximi iussu digestus Benedicti Papae XV auctoritate promulgatus,* Romae: Typis Polyglottis Vaticanis, 1917. Reimpressio, 1932.

*Codicis Iuris Canonici Fontes Emi Petri Card. Gasparri editi,* 9 vols., Romae (postea Civitate Vaticana): Typis Polyglottis Vaticanis, 1923-1939. (Vols. VII, VIII, et IX ed. cura et studio Emi Iustiniani Card. Serédi.)

*Codificazione Canonica Orientale,* Romae: Typografia Poliglotta Vaticana, 1930—. Fascicolo I, *Testi Vari di Diritto Nuovo.* Fascicolo IX, *Disciplina Generalis.* Fascicolo XI, *Ius Particulare Ruthenorum.* Fascicolo XII, *Ius Particulare Maronitarum.* Fascicolo XV, *Droit Particulier des Melkites* (1724-1932). Series II, Fascicolo XXVII, *Disciplina Antiochena Antica—Siri.*

*Collectanea Sacrae Congregationis de Propaganda Fide,* 2 vols., Romae, 1907.

*Corpus Iuris Canonici,* ed. Lipsiensis secunda, post Aemelii Ludovici Richteri curas instruxit Aemelius Friedberg, 2 vols., Lipsiae: Ex Officina Bernhardi Tauchnitz, 1879-1881. Editio anastatice repetita, Lipsiae, 1922.

*Corpus Scriptorum Ecclesiasticorum Latinorum,* Vindobonae; F. Tempsky, 1866—.

*Enchiridion Smybolorum Definitionum et Declarationum de Rebus Fidei et Morum,* Denzinger-Bannwart-Umberg, ed. 21-23, St. Louis: Herder & Co., 1937.

Hardouin, Jean, *Acta Conciliorum et Epistolae Decretales ac Constitutiones Summorum Pontificum,* 12 vols., Parisiis, 1714-1715.

*Historia Ecclesiastica, Die griechischen christlichen Schriftsteller der ersten drei Jahrhunderte,* 7 vols. in 10, ed. Schwartz, Leipzig, 1902-1926, *Eusebius Werke,* Vol. II, pars 1, 1903 and Vol. II, pars 2, 1908.

Jaffé, Philippus, *Regesta Pontificum Romanorum ab condita Ecclesia ad annum post Christum natum MCXCVIII (1198),* 2. ed., cura Wattenbach, Kaltenbrunner (ad annum 590), Ewald (anno 590-882), Löwenfeld (anno 882-1198), 2 vols., Lipsiae, 1885-1888.

Mansi, Joannes D., *Sacrorum Conciliorum Nova et Amplissima Collectio,* 53 vols. in 60, Paris, 1901-1927.

Potthast, Augustus, *Regesta Pontificum Romanorum inde ab anno post Christum natum MCXCVIII (1198) ad annum MCCCIV (1304)*, 2 vols., Berolini, 1874-1875.

Quasten, Johannes, *Monumenta Eucharistica et Liturgica Vetustissima*, Bonnae: Petrus Hanstein, 1935.

*Synodus Alexandrina Coptorum habiti [a?] Cairi in Aegypto anno 1898*, Romae: Typis Polyglottis S. C. de Prop. Fide, 1899.

*Synodus Sciarfensis Syrorum in Monte Libano Celebrata anno 1888*, Romae: Typis Polyglottis S. C. de Prop. Fide, 1896.

Thiel, Andreas, *Epistolae Romanorum Pontificum a Sancto Hilario (461-468) usque ad Sanctum Hormisdam (514-523)*, Brunsbergae, 1868.

## Reference Works

Alphonsus de Liguori, *Theologia Moralis*, 2 vols., Romae: Augustae Taurinorum ex typis H. Marietti, 1891.

Alzog, John, *Universal Church History*, translated, with additions, from the ninth and last German edition by the Rev. F. J. Pabisch and the Rev. Thomas S. Byrne, 4 vols., Dublin, 1874.

Aquinas, St. Thomas, *Summa Theologica*, 6 vols., Taurini, 1886.

Attwater, Donald, *The Catholic Eastern Churches*, 2. ed., Milwaukee: Bruce Publishing Company, 1937.

Augustine, Charles, *A Commentary on the New Code of Canon Law*, 8 vols., St. Louis: B. Herder Book Co., Vol. IV, 3. ed., 1925, and Vol. VI, 3. ed., 1931.

Ayrinhac, H. A., *Administrative Legislation in the New Code of Canon Law*, New York: Longmans, Green & Co., 1930.

Beste, Udalricus, *Introductio in Codicem*, 2. ed., Collegeville, Minn.: St. John's Abbey Press, 1944.

Blat, Albertus, *Commentarium Textus Codicis Iuris Canonici*, 5 vols. in 6, Romae: ex Typographia Pontificia in Instituto Pii IX, Vol. III, Pars I, *De Sacramentis*, 1920.

Bona, Joannes, *Rerum Liturgicarum Libri Duo*, Romae, 1671.

Cappello, Felix M., *Tractatus Canonico-Moralis de Sacramentis*, 3 vols. in 6, Romae: Marietti, Vol. I, *De Sacramentis in Genere, de Baptismo, Confirmatione et Eucharistia*, 4. ed., 1945.

Cicognani, Hamletus I., *Commentarium ad Librum I Codicis*, Romae: ex Schola Typographica "Pio X," 1925.

Collins, Harold E., *The Church Edifice and Its Appointments*, Philadelphia: The Dolphin Press, 1936.

Davis, Henry, *Moral and Pastoral Theology*, 4. ed., 4 vols., New York: Sheed & Ward, 1943. Vol. III.

De Puniet, Dom Jean, *The Mass: Its Origin and History*, translated by the Benedictines of Stanbrook, New York: Longmans, Green & Co., 1930.

Duchesne, Louis, *Christian Worship: Its Origin and Evolution*, translated from the third French edition by M. L. McClure, London: Society for Promoting Christian Knowledge, 1903.

Duskie, John A., *The Canonical Status of the Orientals in the United States*, The Catholic University of America Canon Law Studies, n. 48, Washington, D. C.: The Catholic University of America, 1928.

Eusebius, *Church History*, translated into English with Prolegomena and Explanatory Notes under the Editorial Supervision of Henry Wace and Philip Schaff, 2 vols., New York, 1890.

Fortescue, Adrian, *The Mass: A Study of the Roman Liturgy*, New York: Longmans, Green & Co., 1930.

———, *The Orthodox Eastern Church*, London: Catholic Truth Society, 1907.

———, *The Uniate Eastern Churches*, New York: Benziger Brothers, 1923.

Funk, Francis X., *A Manual of Church History*, translated by P. Perciballi and edited by W. H. Kent, O.S.C., 2 vols., London: Burns, Oates & Washbourne, Ltd., 1938.

———, *Didascalia et Constitutiones Apostolorum*, 2 vols., Paderborn, 1905.

Gasparri, Petrus, *Tractatus Canonicus de Sanctissima Eucharistia*, 2 vols., Paris, 1897.

Genicot, Eduardus-Salsmans, I., *Institutiones Theologiae Moralis*, 12. ed., 2 vols., Bruxellis: L'Edition Universele, S. A., 1936.

Gihr, Nicholas, *The Holy Sacrifice of the Mass*, 12. ed., St. Louis: B. Herder Book Co., 1937.

Goar, Jacobus, *Euchologion sive Rituale Graecorum Complectens Ritus et Ordines*, Parisiis, 1647.

Hefele, Carolus, et Leclercq, Henricus, *Histoire des Conciles*, 10 tomes in 19 vols., Paris, 1907-1938.

Hore, A. H., *Eighteen Centuries of the Orthodox Greek Church*, New York, 1899.

Husslein, Joseph, *The Mass of the Apostles*, New York: P. J. Kenedy & Sons, 1929.

Jone, *Gesetzbuch des kanonischen Rechtes*, 3 vols., Pederborn: Ferdinand Schoeningh, 1939-1940. Vol. II, 1940.

King, Archdale, *Notes on the Catholic Liturgies*, New York: Longmans, Green & Co., 1930.

Lehmkuhl, Augustinus, *Theologia Moralis*, 11. ed., 2 vols., Friburgi Brisgoviae: Herder & Co., 1910. Vol. II.

Meagher, James, *The Seven Gates of Heaven*, 7. ed., New York, 1892.

Merkelbach, Benedictus Henricus, *Summa Theologiae Moralis*, 2. ed., 3 vols., Parisiis: Desclées, DeBrouwer et Soc., 1936. Vol. III.

Michiels, Gommarus, *Normae Generales Juris Canonici*, 2 vols., Lublin-Polonia: Universitas Catholica, 1929.

Migne, Jacques Paul, *Patrologiae Cursus Completus, Series Graeca*, 161 vols. in 164, Parisiis, 1856-1866.

———, *Patrologiae Cursus Completus, Series Latina*, 221 vols., Parisiis, 1844-1864.

Neale, John, *A History of the Holy Eastern Church*, 2 vols., London, 1850.

———, *Translation of the Primitive Liturgies*, London, 1869.

Nilles, Nicolaus, *Symbolae ad Illustrandam Historiam Ecclesiae Orientalis in Terris Coronae S. Stephani*, 2 vols., Oeniponte, 1885.

Noldin, H.-Schmitt, A., *Summa Theologiae Moralis iuxta Codicem Iuris Canonici*, 26. ed., 3 vols., Oeniponte/Lipsiae: Felician Rauch, 1940. Vol. III.

O'Brien, John, *History of the Mass*, New York, 1891.

Papp-Szilagyi, Josephus, *Enchiridion Juris Ecclesiae Orientalis Catholicae*, 2. ed., Magno-Varadini, 1880.

Petrani, Alexius, *De Relatione Iuridica inter Diversas Ritus in Ecclesia Catholica*, Taurini-Romae: Marietti, 1930.

Pitra, Joannes B., *Iuris Ecclesiastici Graecorum Historia et Monumenta*, 2 vols., Romae, 1864.

Prümmer, Dominicus, *Manuale Theologiae Moralis*, 7. ed., 3 vols., Friburgi Brisgoviae: Herder & Co., 1931. Vol. III.

*Religious Bodies, 1936*, Statistics, History, Doctrine, Organization and Work, U. S. Department of Commerce, Bureau of the Census, 2 vols., United States Government Printing Office: Washington, D. C., 1941.

Renaudot, Eusebius, *Liturgiarum Orientalium Collectio*, 2. ed., 2 vols., London, 1847.

Romsée, Tossain J., *Praxis Celebrandi Missam*, 5 vols. in 4, Leodii, 1791.

Salaville, Sévérien, *An Introduction to the Study of Eastern Liturgies*, adapted from the French with a Preface and some Additional Notes by the Very Rev. Msgr. John M. T. Barton, London: Sands & Co., 1938.

Salmanticensium Collegium, *Cursus Theologia Moralis*, 6 tom. in 3, Venetiis, 1728.

Suarez, Franciscus, *Opera Omnia*, 28 vols., Parisiis, 1856-1878. Vol. XX, 1866.

Tanquerey, A., *Synopsis Theologiae Dogmaticae*, 3 vols., Parisiis: Desclée et Socii, Vol. III, 21. ed., 1929.

Thomassinus, Ludovicus, *Vetus et Nova Ecclesiae Disciplina circa Beneficia et Beneficiarios*, 10 vols., Magontiaci, 1787.

Tixeront, J., *History of Dogmas*, translated from the fifth French Edition by H. L. B., 3 vols., St. Louis, Vol. I, 1910.

Van Hove, A., *Commentarium Lovaniense in Codicem Iuris Canonici*, Vol. I, Tom. I, *Prolegomena*, 2. ed., Mechliniae-Romae: H. Dessain, 1945.

Vazquez, Gabriel, *Commentaria ac Disputationes in Tertiam Partem Sancti Thomae*, 3 vols., Lugduni, 1631.

Vermeersch, A.-Creusen, J., *Epitome Iuris Canonici*, 3 vols., Mechliniae-Romae: H. Dessain, Vol. II, 6. ed., 1940.

Wernz, Franciscus X., *Ius Decretalium*, 6 vols., Romae et Prati, 1898-1905.

Will, Cornelius, *Acta et Scripta Quae de Controversiis Ecclesiae Graecae et Latinae Saeculo Undecimo Composita Extant*, Lipsiae et Marpurgi, 1861.

Woywod, Stanislaus, *A Practical Commentary on the Code of Canon Law*, 7. ed., edited by Callistus Smith, 2 vols., New York: Joseph F. Wagner, 1943. Vol. I.

PERIODICALS

*Jurist, The,* Washington, D. C., 1941—
*Orientalia Christiana,* Romae, 1923-1934.
*Traditio,* New York, 1943—

ARTICLES

Gulovich, Stephen C., "Mass and Holy Communion According to the Oriental Rite in a Church of the Latin Rite,"—*The Jurist,* Washington, D. C.: published by the School of Canon Law, The Catholic University of America, 1941—. Vol. II, n. I (January, 1942).

Quasten, Johannes, "Oriental Influence in the Gallican Liturgy,"—*Traditio,* New York: Cosmopolitan Science and Art Service Co., Inc., edited by Johannes Quasten and Stephen Kuttner, 1943.

Spačil, P. Theophilus, "Doctrina Theologiae Orientis Separati de Sanctissima Eucharistia,"—*Orientalia Christiana,* 36 vols., Romae: Pontificium Institutum Orientalium Studiorum, 1923-1934. Vol. XIII (1928) and Vol. XIV (1929).

# ABBREVIATIONS

*AAS*—*Acta Apostolicae Sedis.*
*Collect.*—*Collectanea Sacrae Congregationis de Propaganda Fide.*
*Coll. Lac.*—*Collectio Lacensis.*
*CSEL*—*Corpus Scriptorum Ecclesiasticorum Latinorum.*
*Fontes*—*Codicis Iuris Canonici Fontes.*
*Fonti*—*Codificazione Canonica Orientale.*
*GCS*—*Die griechischen christlichen Schriftsteller der ersten drei Jahrhunderte.*
Hardouin—*Acta Conciliorum et Epistolae Decretales ac Constitutiones Summorum Pontificum.*
Jaffé—*Regesta Pontificum Romanorum.*
Mansi—*Sacrorum Conciliorum Nova et Amplissima Collectio.*
*MPG*—Migne, *Patrologia Graeca.*
*MPL*—Migne, *Patrologia Latina.*
Potthast—*Regesta Pontificum Romanorum.*
S. C. de Prop. Fide—Sacra Congregatio de Propaganda Fide.
S. C. Or.—Sacra Congregatio Orientalis.
S. C. S. Off.—Suprema Congregatio Sancti Officii.

# ALPHABETICAL INDEX

# INDEX OF CANONS

## BIOGRAPHICAL NOTE

JOSEPH ARTHUR HENRY was born February 9, 1917, in Philadelphia, Pennsylvania. After completing his primary education in Saint Aloysius' Parochial School, he attended La Salle College High School, Philadelphia. In September, 1934, he entered the Theological Seminary of Saint Charles Borromeo, Overbrook, Philadelphia, Pennsylvania, where he received the degree of Bachelor of Arts in June, 1939. He was ordained to the Sacred Priesthood by Dennis Cardinal Dougherty at Philadelphia, Pennsylvania, on May 29, 1943. In September of the same year he entered the School of Canon Law at the Catholic University of America, where he received the degree of the Baccalaureate in Canon Law in May, 1944, and the degree of the Licentiate in Canon Law in May, 1945.

# CANON LAW STUDIES *

1. Freriks, Rev. Celestine A., C.PP.S., J.C.D., Religious Congregations in Their External Relations, 121 pp., 1916.
2. Galliher, Rev. Daniel M., O.P., J.C.D., Canonical Elections, 117 pp., 1917.
3. Borkowski, Rev. Aurelius L., O.F.M., J.C.D., De Confraternitatibus Ecclesiasticis, 136 pp., 1918.
4. Castillo, Rev. Cayo, J.C.D., Disertacion Historico-Canonica sobre la Potestad del Cabildo en Sede Vacante o Impedida del Vicario Capitular, 99 pp., 1919 (1918).
5. Kubelbeck, Rev. William J., S.T.B., J.C.D., The Sacred Penitentiaria and Its Relation to Faculties of Ordinaries and Priests, 129 pp., 1918.
6. Petrovits, Rev. Joseph, J.C., S.T.D., J.C.D., The New Church Law on Matrimony, X-461 pp., 1919.
7. Hickey, Rev. John J., S.T.B., J.C.D., Irregularities and Simple Impediments in the New Code of Canon Law, 100 pp., 1920.
8. Klekotka, Rev. Peter J., S.T.B., J.C.D., Diocesan Consultors, 179 pp., 1920.
9. Wanenmacher, Rev. Francis, J.C.D., The Evidence in Ecclesiastical Procedure Affecting the Marriage Bond, 1920 (Printed 1935).
10. Golden, Rev. Henry Francis, J.C.D., Parochial Benefices in the New Code, IV-119 pp., 1921 (Printed 1925).
11. Koudelka, Rev. Charles J., J.C.D., Pastors, Their Rights and Duties According to the New Code of Canon Law, 211 pp., 1921.
12. Melo, Rev. Antonius, O.F.M., J.C.D., De Exemptione Regularium, X-188 pp., 1921.
13. Schaaf, Rev. Valentine Theodore, O.F.M., S.T.B., J.C.D., The Cloister, X-180 pp., 1921.
14. Burke, Rev. Thomas Joseph, S.T.D., J.C.D., Competence in Ecclesiastical Tribunals, IV-117 pp., 1922.
15. Leech, Rev. George Leo, J.C.D., A Comparative Study of the Constitution "Apostolicae Sedis" and the "Codex Juris Canonici," 179 pp., 1922.
16. Motry, Rev. Hubert Louis, S.T.D., J.C.D., Diocesan Faculties According to the Code of Canon Law, II-167 pp., 1922.
17. Murphy, Rev. George Lawrence, J.C.D., Delinquencies and Penalties in the Administration and the Reception of the Sacraments, IV-121 pp., 1923.
18. O'Reilly, Rev. John Anthony, S.T.B., J.C.D., Ecclesiastical Sepulture in the New Code of Canon Law, II-129 pp., 1923.

---

* From nn. 1-100 inclusive only nn. 25 and 57 are still obtainable.
From n. 101 onward all numbers are available except the following: nn. 101-118 inclusive, and also n. 122.

19. Michalicka, Rev. Wenceslas Cyrill, O.S.B., J.C.D., Judicial Procedure in Dismissal of Clerical Exempt Religious, 107 pp., 1923.
20. Dargin, Rev. Edward Vincent, S.T.B., J.C.D., Reserved Cases According to the Code of Canon Law, IV-103 pp., 1924.
21. Godfrey, Rev. John A., S.T.B., J.C.D., The Right of Patronage According to the Code of Canon Law, 153 pp., 1924.
22. Hagedorn, Rev. Francis Edward, J.C.D., General Legislation on Indulgences, II-154 pp., 1924.
23. King, Rev. James Ignatius, J.C.D., The Administration of the Sacraments to Dying Non-Catholics, V-141 pp., 1924.
24. Winslow, Rev. Francis Joseph, O.F.M., J.C.D., Vicars and Prefects Apostolic, IV-149 pp., 1924.
25. Correa, Rev. Jose Servelion, S.T.L., J.C.D., La Potestad Legislativa de la Iglesia Catolica, IV-127 pp., 1925.
26. Dugan, Rev. Henry Francis, A.M., J.C.D., The Judiciary Department of the Diocesan Curia, 87 pp., 1925.
27. Keller, Rev. Charles Frederick, S.T.B., J.C.D., Mass Stipends, 167 pp., 1925.
28. Paschang, Rev. John Linus, J.C.D., The Sacramentals According to the Code of Canon Law, 129 pp., 1925.
29. Piontek, Rev. Cyrillus, O.F.M., S.T.B., J.C.D., De Indulto Exclaustrationis necnon Saecularizationis, XIII-289 pp., 1925.
30. Kearney, Rev. Richard Joseph, S.T.B., J.C.D., Sponsors at Baptism According to the Code of Canon Law, IV-127 pp., 1925.
31. Bartlett, Rev. Chester Joseph, A.M., LL.B., J.C.D., The Tenure of Parochial Property in the United States of America, V-108 pp., 1926.
32. Kilker, Rev. Adrian Jerome, J.C.D., Extreme Unction, V-425 pp., 1926.
33. McCormick, Rev. Robert Emmett, J.C.D., Confessors of Religious, VIII-266 pp., 1926.
34. Miller, Rev. Newton Thomas, J.C.D., Founded Masses According to the Code of Canon Law, VII-93 pp., 1926.
35. Roelker, Rev. Edward G., S.T.D., J.C.D., Principles of Privilege According to the Code of Canon Law, XI-166 pp., 1926.
36. Bakalarczyk, Rev. Richardus, M.I.C., J.U.D., De Novitiatu, VIII-208 pp., 1927.
37. Pizzuti, Rev. Lawrence, O.F.M., J.U.L., De Parochis Religiosis, 1927. (Not Printed.)
38. Bliley, Rev. Nicholas Martin, O.S.B., J.C.D., Altars According to the Code of Canon Law, XIX-132 pp., 1927.
39. Brown, Mr. Brendan Francis, A.B., LL.M., J.U.D., The Canonical Juristic Personality with Special Reference to its Status in the United States of America, V-212 pp., 1927.
40. Cavanaugh, Rev. William Thomas, C.P., J.U.D., The Reservation of the Blessed Sacrament, VIII-101 pp., 1927.

41. Doheny, Rev. William J., C.S.C., A.B., J.U.D., Church Property: Modes of Acquisition, X-118 pp., 1927.
42. Feldhaus, Rev. Aloysius H., C.PP.S., J.C.D., Oratories, IX-141 pp., 1927.
43. Kelly, Rev. James Patrick, A.B., J.C.D., The Jurisdiction of the Simple Confessor, X-208 pp., 1927.
44. Neuberger, Rev. Nicholas J., J.C.D., Canon 6 or the Relation of the Codex Juris Canonici to the Preceding Legislation, V-95 pp., 1927.
45. O'Keefe, Rev. Gerald Michael, J.C.D., Matrimonial Dispensations, Powers of Bishops, Priests, and Confessors, VIII-232 pp., 1927.
46. Quigley, Rev. Joseph A. M., A.B., J.C.D., Condemned Societies, 139 pp., 1927.
47. Zaplotnik, Rev. Johannes Leo, J.C.D., De Vicariis Foraneis, X-142 pp., 1927.
48. Duskie, Rev. John Aloysius, A.B., J.C.D., The Canonical Status of the Orientals in the United States, VIII-196 pp., 1928.
49. Hyland, Rev. Francis Edward, J.C.D., Excommunication, Its Nature, Historical Development and Effects, VIII-181 pp., 1928.
50. Reinmann, Rev. Gerald Joseph, O.M.C., J.C.D., The Third Order Secular of Saint Francis, 201 pp., 1928.
51. Schenk, Rev. Francis J., J.C.D., The Matrimonial Impediments of Mixed Religion and Disparity of Cult, XVI-318 pp., 1929.
52. Coady, Rev. John Joseph, S.T.D., J.U.D., A.M., The Appointment of Pastors, VIII-150 pp., 1929.
53. Kay, Rev. Thomas Henry, J.C.D., Competence in Matrimonial Procedure, VIII-164 pp., 1929.
54. Turner, Rev. Sidney Joseph, C.P., J.U.D., The Vow of Poverty, XLIX-217 pp., 1929.
55. Kearney, Rev. Raymond A., A.B., S.T.D., J.C.D., The Principles of Delegation, VII-149 pp., 1929.
56. Conran, Rev. Edward James, A.B., J.C.D., The Interdict, V-163 pp., 1930.
57. O'Neill, Rev. William H., J.C.D., Papal Rescripts of Favor, VII-218 pp., 1930.
58. Bastnagel, Rev. Clement Vincent, J.U.D., The Appointment of Parochial Adjutants and Assistants, XV-257 pp., 1930.
59. Ferry, Rev. William A., A.B., J.C.D., Stole Fees, V-136 pp., 1930.
60. Costello, Rev. John Michael, A.B., J.C.D., Domicile and Quasi-Domicile, VII-201 pp., 1930.
61. Kremer, Rev. Michael Nicholas, A.B., S.T.B., J.C.D., Church Support in the United States, VI-136 pp., 1930.
62. Angulo, Rev. Luis, C.M., J.C.D., Legislation de la Iglesia sobre la intencion en la application de la Santa Misa, VII-104 pp., 1931.
63. Frey, Rev. Wolfgang Norbert, O.S.B., A.B., J.C.D., The Act of Religious Profession, VIII-174 pp., 1931.

64. Roberts, Rev. James Brendan, A.B., J.C.D., The Banns of Marriage, XIV-140 pp., 1931.
65. Ryder, Rev. Raymond Aloysius, A.B., J.C.D., Simony, IX-151 pp., 1931.
66. Campagna, Rev. Angelo, Ph.D., J.U.D., Il Vicario Generale del Vescovo, VII-205 pp., 1931.
67. Cox, Rev. Joseph Godfrey, A.B., J.C.D., The Administration of Seminaries, VI-124 pp., 1931.
68. Gregory, Rev. Donald J., J.U.D., The Pauline Privilege, XV-165 pp., 1931.
69. Donohue, Rev. John F., J.C.D., The Impediment of Crime, VII-110 pp., 1931.
70. Dooley, Rev. Eugene A., O.M.I., J.C.D., Church Law on Sacred Relics, IX-143 pp., 1931.
71. Orth, Rev. Clement Raymond, O.M.C., J.C.D., The Approbation of Religious Institutes, 171 pp., 1931.
72. Pernicone, Rev. Joseph M., A.B., J.C.D., The Ecclesiastical Prohibition of Books, XII-267 pp., 1932.
73. Clinton, Rev. Connell, A.B., J.C.D., The Paschal Precept, IX-108 pp., 1932.
74. Donnelly, Rev. Francis B., A.M., S.T.L., J.C.D., The Diocesan Synod, VIII-125 pp., 1932.
75. Torrente, Rev. Camilo, C.M.F., J.C.D., Las Procesiones Sagradas, V-145 pp., 1932.
76. Murphy, Rev. Edwin J., C.PP.S., J.C.D., Suspension Ex Informata Conscientia, XI-122 pp., 1932.
77. MacKenzie, Rev. Eric F., A.M., S.T.L., J.C.D., The Delict of Heresy in its Commission, Penalization, Absolution, VII-124 pp., 1932.
78. Lyons, Rev. Avitus E., S.T.B., J.C.D., The Collegiate Tribunal of First Instance, XI-147 pp., 1932.
79. Connolly, Rev. Thomas A., J.C.D., Appeals, XI-195, pp., 1932.
80. Sangmeister, Rev. Joseph V., A.B., J.C.D., Force and Fear as Precluding Matrimonial Consent, V-211 pp., 1932.
81. Jaeger, Rev. Leo A., A.B., J.C.D., The Administration of Vacant and Quasi-Vacant Episcopal Sees in the United States, IX-229 pp., 1932.
82. Rimlinger, Rev. Herbert T., J.C.D., Error Invalidating Matrimonial Consent, VII-79 pp., 1932.
83. Barrett, Rev. John D. M., S.S., J.C.D., A Comparative Study of the Third Plenary Council of Baltimore and the Code, IX-221 pp., 1932.
84. Carberry, Rev. John J., Ph.D., S.T.D., J.C.D., The Juridical Form of Marriage, X-177 pp., 1934.
85. Dolan, Rev. John L., A.B., J.C.D., The Defensor Vinculi, XII-157 pp., 1934.
86. Hannan, Rev. Jerome D., A.M., S.T.D., LL.B., J.C.D., The Canon Law of Wills, IX-517 pp., 1934.

87. LEMIEUX, REV. DELISE A., A.M., J.C.D., The Sentence in Ecclesiastical Procedure, IX-131 pp., 1934.
88. O'ROURKE, REV. JAMES J., A.B., J.C.D., Parish Registers, VII-109 pp., 1934.
89. TIMLIN, REV. BARTHOLOMEW, O.F.M., A.M., J.C.D., Conditional Matrimonial Consent, X-381 pp., 1934.
90. WAHL, REV. FRANCIS X., A.B., J.C.D., The Matrimonial Impediments of Consanguinity and Affinity, VI-125 pp., 1934.
91. WHITE, REV. ROBERT J., A.B., LL.B., S.T.B., J.C.D., Canonical Ante-Nuptial Promises and the Civil Law, VI-152 pp., 1934.
92. HERRERA, REV. ANTONIO PARRA, O.C.D., J.C.D., Legislacion Ecclesiastica sobra el Ayuno y la Abstinencia, XI-191 pp., 1935.
93. KENNEDY, REV. EDWIN J., J.C.D., The Special Matrimonial Process in Cases of Evident Nullity, X-165 pp., 1935.
94. MANNING, REV. JOHN J., A.B., J.C.D., Presumption of Law in Matrimonial Procedure, XI-111 pp., 1935.
95. MOEDER, REV. JOHN M., J.C.D., The Proper Bishop for Ordination and Dismissorial Letters, VII-135 pp., 1935.
96. O'MARA, REV. WILLIAM A., A.B., J.C.D., Canonical Causes for Matrimonial Dispensations, IX-155 pp., 1935.
97. REILLY, REV. PETER, J.C.D., Residence of Pastors, IX-81 pp., 1935.
98. SMITH, REV. MARINER T., O.P., S.T.Lr., J.C.D., The Penal Law for Religious, VIII-169 pp., 1935.
99. WHALEN, REV. DONALD W., A.M., J.C.D., The Value of Testimonial Evidence in Matrimonial Procedure, XIII-297 pp., 1935.
100. CLEARY, REV. JOSEPH F., J.C.D., Canonical Limitations on the Alienation of Church Property, VIII-141 pp., 1936.
101. GLYNN, REV. JOHN C., J.C.D., The Promoter of Justice, XX-337 pp., 1936.
102. BRENNAN, REV. JAMES H., S.S., M.A., S.T.B., J.C.D., The Simple Convalidation of Marriage, VI-135 pp., 1937.
103. BRUNINI, REV. JOSEPH BERNARD, J.C.D., The Clerical Obligations of Canons 139 and 142, X-121 pp., 1937.
104. CONNOR, REV. MAURICE, A.B., J.C.D., The Administrative Removal of Pastors, VIII-159 pp., 1937.
105. GUILFOYLE, REV. MERLIN JOSEPH, J.C.D., Custom, XI-144 pp., 1937.
106. HUGHES, REV. JAMES AUSTIN, A.B., A.M., J.C.D., Witnesses in Criminal Trials of Clerics, IX-140 pp., 1937.
107. JANSEN, REV. RAYMOND J., A.B., S.T.L., J.C.D., Canonical Provisions for Catechetical Instruction, VII-153 pp., 1937.
108. KEALY, REV. JOHN JAMES, A.B., J.C.D., The Introductory Libellus in Church Court Procedure, XI-121 pp., 1937.
109. McMANUS, REV. JAMES EDWARD, C.SS.R., J.C.D., The Administration of Temporal Goods in Religious Institutes, XVI-196 pp., 1937.

110. Moriarty, Rev. Eugene James, J.C.D., Oaths in Ecclesiastical Courts, X-115 pp., 1937.

111. Rainer, Rev. Eligius George, C.SS.R., J.C.D., Suspension of Clerics, XVII-249 pp., 1937.

112. Reilly, Rev. Thomas F., C.SS.R., J.C.D., Visitation of Religious, VI-195 pp., 1938.

113. Moriarty, Rev. Francis E., C.SS.R., J.C.D., The Extraordinary Absolution from Censures, XV-334 pp., 1938.

114. Connolly, Rev. Nicholas P., J.C.D., The Canonical Erection of Parishes, X-132 pp., 1938.

115. Donovan, Rev. James Joseph, J.C.D., The Pastor's Obligation in Prenuptial Investigation, XII-322 pp., 1938.

116. Harrigan, Rev. Robert J., M.A., S.T.B., J.C.D., The Radical Sanation of Invalid Marriages, VIII-208 pp., 1938.

117. Boffa, Rev. Conrad Humbert, J.C.D., Canonical Provisions for Catholic Schools, VII-211 pp., 1939.

118. Parsons, Rev. Anscar John, O.M.Cap., J.C.D., Canonical Elections, XII-236 pp., 1939.

119. Reilly, Rev. Edward Michael, A.B., J.C.D., The General Norms of Dispensation, XII-156 pp., 1939.

120. Ryan, Rev. Gerald Aloysius, A.B., J.C.D., Principles of Episcopal Jurisdiction, XII-172 pp., 1939.

121. Burton, Rev. Francis James, C.S.C., A.B., J.C.D., A Commentary on Canon 1125, X-222 pp., 1940.

122. Miaskiewicz, Rev. Francis Sigismund, J.C.D., Supplied Jurisdiction According to Canon 209, XII-340 pp., 1940.

123. Rice, Rev. Patrick William, A.B., J.C.D., Proof of Death in Prenuptial Investigation, VIII-156 pp., 1940.

124. Anglin, Rev. Thomas Francis, M.S., J.C.D., The Eucharistic Fast, VIII-183 pp., 1941.

125. Coleman, Rev. John Jerome, J.C.D., The Minister of Confirmation, VI-153 pp., 1941.

126. Downs, Rev. John Emmanuel, A.B., J.C.D., The Concept of Clerical Immunity, XI-163 pp., 1941.

127. Esswein, Rev. Anthony Albert, J.C.D., Extrajudicial Penal Powers of Ecclesiastical Superiors, X-144 pp., 1941.

128. Farrell, Rev. Benjamin Francis, M.A., S.T.L., J.C.D., The Rights and Duties of the Local Ordinary Regarding Congregations of Women Religious of Pontifical Approval, V-195 pp., 1941.

129. Feeney, Rev. Thomas John, A.B., S.T.L., J.C.D., Restitutio in Integrum, VI-169 pp., 1941.

130. Findlay, Rev. Stephen William, O.S.B., A.B., J.C.D., Canonical Norms Governing the Deposition and Degradation of Clerics, XVII-279 pp., 1941.

131. Goodwine, Rev. John, A.B., S.T.L., J.C.D., The Right of the Church to Acquire Property, VIII-119 pp., 1941.
132. Heston, Rev. Edward Louis, C.S.C., Ph.D., S.T.D., J.C.D., The Alienation of Church Property in the United States, XII-222 pp., 1941.
133. Hogan, Rev. James John, A.B., S.T.L., J.C.D., Judicial Advocates and Procurators, XIII-200 pp., 1941.
134. Kealy, Rev. Thomas M., A.B., Litt.B., J.C.D., Dowry of Women Religious, IX-152 pp., 1941.
135. Keene, Rev. Michael James, O.S.B., J.C.D., Religious Ordinaries and Canon 198, V-164 pp., 1942.
136. Kerin, Rev. Charles A., S.S., M.A., S.T.B., J.C.D., The Privation of Christian Burial, XVI-279 pp., 1941.
137. Louis, Rev. William Francis, M.A., J.C.D., Diocesan Archives, X-101 pp., 1941.
138. McDevitt, Rev. Gilbert Joseph, A.B., J.C.D., Legitimacy and Legitimation, X-247 pp., 1941.
139. McDonough, Rev. Thomas Joseph, A.B., J.C.D., Apostolic Administrators, X-217 pp., 1941.
140. Meier, Rev. Carl Anthony, A.B., J.C.D., Penal Administrative Procedure Against Negligent Pastors, XI-240 pp., 1941.
141. Schmidt, Rev. John Rogg, A.B., J.C.D., The Principles of Authentic Interpretation in Canon 17 of the Code of Canon Law, XII-331 pp., 1941.
142. Slafkosky, Rev. Andrew Leonard, A.B., J.C.D., The Canonical Episcopal Visitation of the Diocese, X-197 pp., 1941.
143. Swoboda, Rev. Innocent Robert, O.F.M., J.C.D., Ignorance in Relation to the Imputability of Delicts, IX-271 pp., 1941.
144. Dubé, Rev. Arthur Joseph, A.B., J.C.D., The General Principles for the Reckoning of Time in Canon Law, VIII-299 pp., 1941.
145. McBride, Rev. James T., A.B., J.C.D., Incardination and Excardination of Seculars, XX-585 pp., 1941.
146. Król, Rev. John T., J.C.D., The Defendant in Ecclesiastical Trials, XII-207 pp., 1942.
147. Comyns, Rev. Joseph J., C.SS.R., A.B., J.C.D., Papal and Episcopal Administration of Church Property, XIV-155 pp., 1942.
148. Barry, Rev. Garrett Francis, O.M.I., J.C.D., Violation of the Cloister, XII-260 pp., 1942.
149. Bolduc, Rev. Gatien, C.S.V., A.B., S.T.L., J.C.D., Les Études dans les Religions Cléricales, VIII-155 pp., 1942.
150. Boyle, Rev. David John, M.A., J.C.D., The Juridic Effects of Moral Certitude on Pre-Nuptial Guarantees, XII-188 pp., 1942.
151. Canavan, Rev. Walter Joseph, M.A., Litt.D., J.C.D., The Profession of Faith, XII-143 pp., 1942.
152. Desrochers, Rev. Bruno, A.B., Ph.L., S.T.B., J.C.D., Le Premier Concile Plénier de Québec et le Code de Droit Canonique, XIV-186 pp., 1942.

153. Dillon, Rev. Robert Edward, A.B., J.C.D., Common Law Marriage, X-148 pp., 1942.
154. Dodwell, Rev. Edward John, Ph.D., S.T.B., J.C.D., The Time and Place for the Celebration of Marriage, X-156 pp., 1942.
155. Donnellan, Rev. Thomas Andrew, A.B., J.C.D., The Obligation of the Missa pro Populo, VII-131 pp., 1942.
156. Eltz, Rev. Louis Anthony, A.B., J.C.D., Cooperation in Crime, XII-208 pp., 1942.
157. Gass, Rev. Sylvester Francis, M.A., J.C.D., Ecclesiastical Pensions, XI-206 pp., 1942.
158. Guiniven, Rev. John Joseph, C.SS.R., J.C.D., The Precept of Hearing Mass, XIV-188 pp., 1942.
159. Gulczynski, Rev. John Theophilus, J.C.D., The Desecration and Violation of Churches, X-126 pp., 1942.
160. Hammill, Rev. John Leo, M.A., J.C.D., The Obligations of the Traveler According to Canon 14, VIII-204 pp., 1942.
161. Haydt, Rev. John Joseph, A.B., J.C.D., Reserved Benefices, XI-148 pp., 1942.
162. Huser, Rev. Roger John, O.F.M., A.B., J.C.D., The Crime of Abortion in Canon Law, XII-187 pp., 1942.
163. Kearney, Rev. Francis Patrick, A.B., S.T.L., J.C.D., The Principles of Canon 1127, X-162 pp., 1942.
164. Linahen, Rev. Leo James, S.T.L., J.C.D., De Absolutione Complicis in Peccato Turpi, V-114 pp., 1942.
165. McCloskey, Rev. Joseph Aloysius, A.B., J.C.D., The Subject of Ecclesiastical Law According to Canon 12, XVII-246 pp., 1942.
166. O'Neill, Rev. Francis Joseph, C.SS.R., J.C.D., The Dismissal of Religious in Temporary Vows, XIII-220 pp., 1942.
167. Prince, Rev. John Edward, A.B., S.T.B., J.C.D., The Diocesan Chancellor, X-136 pp., 1942.
168. Riesner, Rev. Albert Joseph, C.SS.R., J.C.D., Apostates and Fugitives from Religious Institutes, IX-168 pp., 1942.
169. Stenger, Rev. Joseph Bernard, J.C.D., The Mortgaging of Church Property, 186 pp., 1942.
170. Waldron, Rev. Joseph Francis, A.B., J.C.D., The Minister of Baptism, XII-197 pp., 1942.
171. Willett, Rev. Robert Albert, J.C.D., The Probative Value of Documents in Ecclesiastical Trials, X-124 pp., 1942.
172. Woeber, Rev. Edward Martin, M.A., J.C.D., The Interpellations, XII-161 pp., 1942.
173. Benko, Rev. Matthew Aloysius, O.S.B., M.A., J.C.D., The Abbot *Nullius*, XVI-148 pp., 1943.
174. Christ, Rev. Joseph James, M.A., S.T.L., J.C.D., Dispensation from Vindicative Penalties, XIV-285 pp., 1943.

175. CLANCY, REV. PATRICK M. J., O.P., A.B., S.T.Lr., J.C.D., The Local Religious Superior, X-229 pp., 1943.
176. CLARKE, REV. THOMAS JAMES, J.C.D., Parish Societies, XII-147 pp., 1943.
177. CONNOLLY, REV. JOHN PATRICK, S.T.L., J.C.D., Synodal Examiners and Parish Priest Consultors, X-223 pp., 1943.
178. DRUMM, REV. WILLIAM MARTIN, A.B., J.C.D., Hospital Chaplains, XII-175 pp., 1943.
179. FLANAGAN, REV. BERNARD JOSEPH, A.B., S.T.L., J.C.D., The Canonical Erection of Religious Houses, X-147 pp., 1943.
180. KELLEHER, REV. STEPHEN JOSEPH, A.B., S.T.B., J.C.D., Discussions with Non-Catholics: Canonical Legislation, X-93 pp., 1943.
181. LEWIS, REV. GORDIAN, C.P., J.C.D., Chapters in Religious Institutes, XII-169 pp., 1943.
182. MARX, REV. ADOLPH, J.C.D., The Declaration of Nullity of Marriages Contracted Outside the Church, X-151 pp., 1943.
183. MATULENAS, REV. RAYMOND ANTHONY, O.S.B., A.B., J.C.D., Communication, a Source of Privileges, XII-225 pp., 1943.
184. O'LEARY, REV. CHARLES GERARD, C.SS.R., J.C.D., Religious Dismissed After Perpetual Profession, X-213 pp., 1943.
185. POWER, REV. CORNELIUS MICHAEL, J.C.D., The Blessing of Cemeteries, XII-231 pp., 1943.
186. SHUHLER, REV. RALPH VINCENT, O.S.A., J.C.D., Privileges of Religious to Absolve and Dispense, XII-195 pp., 1943.
187. ZIOLKOWSKI, REV. THADDEUS STANISLAUS, A.B., J.C.D., The Consecration and Blessing of Churches, XII-151 pp., 1943.
188. HENEGHAN, REV. JOHN JOSEPH, S.T.D., J.C.D., The Marriages of Unworthy Catholics: Canons 1065 and 1066, XVI-213 pp., 1944.
189. CARROLL, REV. COLEMAN FRANCIS, M.A., S.T.L., J.C.L., Charitable Institutions.
190. CIESLUK, REV. JOSEPH EDWARD, PH.B., S.T.L., J.C.L., National Parishes in the United States.
191. COBURN, REV. VINCENT PAUL, A.B., J.C.D., Marriages of Conscience, XII-172 pp., 1944.
192. CONNORS, REV. CHARLES PAUL, C.S.SP., A.B., J.C.D., Extra-Judicial Procurators in the Code of Canon Law, X-94 pp., 1944.
193. COYLE, REV. PAUL RAYMOND, A.B., J.C.D., Judicial Exceptions, X-142 pp., 1944.
194. FAIR, REV. BARTHOLOMEW FRANCIS, A.B., S.T.L., J.C.L., The Impediment of Abduction.
195. GALLAGHER, REV. THOMAS RAPHAEL, O.P., A.B., S.T.LR., J.C.D., The Examination of the Qualities of the Ordinand, X-166 pp., 1944.
196. GANNON, REV. JOHN MARK, S.T.L., J.C.D., The Interstices Required for the Promotion to Orders, XII-100 pp., 1944.

197. GOLDSMITH, REV. J. WILLIAM, B.C.S., S.T.L., J.C.D., The Competence of Church and State Over Marriages—Disputed Points, X-128 pp., 1944.

198. GOODWINE, REV. JOSEPH GERARD, A.B., S.T.B., J.C.D., The Reception of Converts, XIV-326 pp., 1944.

199. KOWALSKI, REV. ROMUALD EUGENE, O.F.M., A.B., J.C.D., Sustenance of Religious Houses of Regulars, X-174 pp., 1944.

200. MCCOY, REV. ALAN EDWARD, O.F.M., J.C.D., Force and Fear in Relation to Delictual Imputability and Penal Responsibility, XII-160 pp., 1944.

201. MCDEVITT, REV. VINCENT JOHN, PH.B., S.T.L., J.C.L., Perjury.

202. MARTIN, REV. THOMAS OWEN, PH.D., S.T.D., J.C.D., Adverse Possession, Prescription and Limitation of Actions: The Canonical "Praescriptio," XX-208 pp., 1944.

203. MIKLOSOVIC, REV. PAUL JOHN, A.B., J.C.L., Attempted Marriages and Their Consequent Juridic Effects.

204. MUNDY, REV. THOMAS MAURICE, A.B., S.T.L., J.C.D., The Union of Parishes, X-164 pp., 1944.

205. O'DEA, REV. JOHN COYLE, A.B., J.C.D., The Matrimonial Impediment of Nonage, VIII-126 pp., 1944.

206. OLALIA, REV. ALEXANDER AYSON, S.T.L., J.C.D., A Comparative Study of the Christian Constitution of States and the Constitution of the Philippine Commonwealth, XII-136 pp., 1944.

207. POISSON, REV. PIERRE-MARIE, C.S.C., A.B., PH.L., TH.L., J.C.L., Droits Patrimoniaux des Maisons et des Eglises Religieuses.

208. STADALNIKAS, REV. CASIMIR JOSEPH, M.I.C., J.C.D., Reservation of Censures, X-141 pp., 1944.

209. SULLIVAN, REV. EUGENE HENRY, S.T.L., J.C.D., Proof of the Reception of the Sacraments, X-165 pp., 1944.

210. VAUGHAN, REV. WILLIAM EDWARD, J.C.D., Constitutions for Diocesan Courts, X-210 pp., 1944.

211. PARO, REV. GINO, S.T.D., J.C.L., The Right of Apostolic Legation.

212. BALZER, REV. RALPH FRANCIS, C.P., J.C.L., The Computation of Time in a Canonical Novitiate.

213. DOUGHERTY, REV. JOHN WHELAN, A.B., S.T.L., J.C.L., De Inquisitione Speciali.

214. DZIOB, REV. MICHAEL WALTER, J.C.L., The Sacred Congregation for the Oriental Church.

215. EIDENSCHINK, REV. JOHN ALBERT, O.S.B., B.A., J.C.L., The Election of Bishops in the Letters of Pope Gregory the Great.

216. GILL, REV. NICHOLAS, C.P., J.C.L., The Spiritual Prefect in Clerical Religious Houses of Study.

217. HYNES, REV. HARRY GERARD, S.T.L., J.C.D., The Privileges of Cardinals, XII-183 pp., 1945.

218. McDevitt, Rev. Gerald Vincent, S.T.L., J.C.D., The Renunciation of an Ecclesiastical Office, XIV-179 pp., 1945.
219. Manning, Rev. Joseph Leroy, J.C.L., The Free Conferral of Offices.
220. Meyer, Rev. Louis G., O.S.B., A.B., S.T.B., J.C.D., Alms-gathering by Religious, XII-163 pp., 1945.
221. O'Donnell, Rev. Cletus Francis, M.A., J.C.L., The Marriage of Minors.
222. Prunskis, Rev. Joseph, J.C.D., Comparative Law, Ecclesiastical and Civil, in Lithuanian Concordat, X-161 pp., 1945.
223. Sweeney, Rev. Francis Patrick, C.SS.R., J.C.D., The Reduction of Clerics to the Lay State, X-199 pp., 1945.
224. Vogelpohl, Rev. Henry John, J.C.L., The Simple Impediments to Holy Orders.
225. Brockhaus, Rev. Thomas Aquinas, O.S.B., J.C.L., Religious who are known as *Conversi*.
226. Griese, Rev. Orville Nicholas, S.T.D., J.C.L., Marriage and the Procreation of Offspring.
227. Boudreaux, Rev. Warren Louis, J.C.L., The "*ab acatholicis nati*" of Canon 1099, § 2.
228. Bowe, Rev. Thomas Joseph, A.B., J.C.L., Religious Superioresses.
229. Diederichs, Rev. Michael Ferdinand, S.C.J., J.C.L., The Jurisdiction of the Latin Ordinaries over their Oriental Subjects.
230. Dingman, Rev. Maurice John, A.B., S.T.L., J.C.L., The Plaintiff in Contentious Trials.
231. Frison, Rev. Basil, C.M.F., M.Mus., J.C.L., The Retroactivity of Law.
232. Galvin, Rev. William Anthony, M.A., J.C.L., The Administrative Transfer of Pastors.
233. Goracy, Rev. Joseph C., J.C.L., The Diriment Matrimonial Impediment of Major Orders.
234. Hale, Rev. Joseph Francis, M.A., S.T.L., J.C.L., The Pastor of Burial.
235. Henry, Rev. Joseph Arthur, A.B., J.C.L., The Mass and Holy Communion: Interritual Law.
236. Linenberger, Rev. Herbert, C.PP.S., J.C.L., The False Denunciation of an Innocent Confessor.
237. Lowry, Rev. James Martin, A.B., J.C.L., Dispensation from Private Vows.
238. Lynch, Rev. George Edward, A.B., S.T.L., J.C.L., Coadjutors and Auxiliaries of Bishops.
239. Lynch, Rev. Timothy, M.S.SS.T., J.C.L., Contracts between Bishops and Religious Congregations.
240. McClunn, Rev. Justin David, A.B., S.T.L., J.C.L., Administrative Recourse.
241. McGarvey, Rev. Thomas Joseph, A.B., S.T.L., J.C.L., Bination.
242. McGrath, Rev. James, A.B., J.C.L., The Privilege of the Canon.
243. Marbach, Rev. Joseph Francis, A.B., J.C.L., Marriage Legislation for the Catholics of the Oriental Rites in the United States and Canada.

244. Shimkus, Rev. Bernard Aloysius, A.B., J.C.L., The Determination and Transfer of Rite.

245. Smith, Rev. Vincent Michael, A.B., S.T.L., J.C.L., Ignorance Affecting Matrimonial Consent.

246. Wachtrle, Rev. Paul Anthony, A.B., J.C.L., The Baptism of the Children of Non-Catholics.

www.ingramcontent.com/pod-product-compliance
Lightning Source LLC
LaVergne TN
LVHW050213080826
844660LV00012B/403
* 9 7 8 0 8 1 3 2 2 4 1 5 2 *